GREENHOUSE

A COMPREHENSIVE GUIDE TO CULTIVATING FRUITS, VEGETABLES, AND HERBS FOR BEGINNERS

BY TOM GORDON

© Copyright 2019 - All rights reserved.

The content contained within this book may not be reproduced, duplicated or transmitted without direct written permission from the author or the publisher.

Under no circumstances will any blame or legal responsibility be held against the publisher, or author, for any damages, reparation, or monetary loss due to the information contained within this book. Either directly or indirectly.

Legal Notice:

This book is copyright protected. This book is only for personal use. You cannot amend, distribute, sell, use, quote or paraphrase any part, or the content within this book, without the consent of the author or publisher.

Disclaimer Notice:

Please note the information contained within this document is for educational and entertainment purposes only. All effort has been executed to present accurate, up to date, and reliable, complete information. No warranties of any kind are declared or implied. Readers acknowledge that the author is not engaging in the rendering of legal, financial, medical or professional advice. The content within this book has been derived from various sources. Please consult a licensed professional before attempting any techniques outlined in this book.

By reading this document, the reader agrees that under no circumstances is the author responsible for any losses, direct or indirect, which are incurred as a result of the use of information contained within this document, including, but not limited to, — errors, omissions, or inaccuracies.

Table of Contents

Introduction x

Chapter One - Greenhouse Gardening 1

Why Cultivate In A Greenhouse 2
Where To Start 4
Site Selection For The Greenhouse 5
Types Of Greenhouses 7

    Lean-To Greenhouse Structure 8

    Even Span Greenhouse Structure 11

    Uneven Span Greenhouse Structure 13

    A-Frame Greenhouse Structure 16

    Quonset Greenhouse Structure/ Hoop-House Structure 17

    Gothic Arch Greenhouse Structure 20

    Ridge And Furrow Greenhouse Structure 22

    Sawtooth Greenhouse Structure 24

Cold Frame Greenhouse Structure........ 25
Hotbed Greenhouse 27
Construction Of The Greenhouse 30
Layout Of The Greenhouse Site................ 35

Chapter Two - Operating A Greenhouse 40

Controlling Temperature Conditions........ 41
Heating 41
Ventilation And Air Flow............................ 42
Lighting.. 45
Humidity.. 45
How To Keep The Greenhouse Warm 46

Chapter Three - Greenhouse Equipment 53

Basic Equipment 54
Furniture To Store Greenhouse Equipment.. 57
Lighting System Equipment 58
Temperature Control And Heating System Equipment 60
Ventilation Equipment............................ 63

Pest Control Equipment 65
Other Greenhouse Accessories 65

Chapter Four - Cultivating Fruits 70

Getting Started With The Seedling Stage . 72

Soil Preparation 73

How To Improve Soil Drainage And Consistency 74

How To Test Soil Nutrients And Ph 77

How To Balance Ph Level And Fertilize The Soil 79

Water Requirements For Planting Fruits .. 82

Mulching The Fruit Tree 85

Fruit Tree Pollination 88

Chapter Five - Cultivating Vegetables 92

Getting Started 93

How To Grow Vegetables In The Greenhouse 94

Challenges You May Face 100

What Vegetables To Plant And When 101

How To Determine The Best Soil For Planting Vegetables 104

    Determining Soil Health 105

    Soil Testing 105

    Soil Texture And Type 107

    Improving Soil 109

Adding Fertilizers To The Soil 111

Watering Vegetables 112

Pollination In Vegetables 115

Chapter Six - Cultivating Herbs 122

Tips For Growing Herbs 124

Basic Requirements For Herb Growth ... 126

How To Grow Herbs From Seeds 128

Soil Preparation 132

Types Of Herbs You Can Grow In A Greenhouse 135

Fertilizing 136

Pollination Of Herbs 138

Watering Herbs 142

How To Know The Herbs Have Been Overwatered................................142

How To Avoid Overwatering..............144

Chapter Seven - Maintaining Your Greenhouse 146

How To Maintain The Greenhouse........147

Weed Control..............................152

How To Prepare Your Greenhouse For The Winter Season.....................156

Chapter Eight - Pests And Disease Control.. 165

Pest Management........................165

Tips For Pest And Disease Control........170

Integrated Pest Management Techniques..................................172

Managing Diseases......................178

Disease Preventive Measures 183

Common Greenhouse Diseases................184

Chapter Nine - Mistakes To Avoid......... 190

Final Words **199**

GREENHOUSE

INTRODUCTION

This comprehensive guide will provide you with a step-by-step procedure for setting up a greenhouse in your own backyard. The tutorial highlights the equipment and tools needed to build and successfully run your greenhouse garden.

As a beginner to greenhouse gardening, you're bound to make many mistakes, and this guide will help you avoid some of the errors made by other greenhouse farmers. You don't have to make the same mistakes while cultivating fruits, vegetables, and herbs in your garden.

You will learn how to manage the greenhouse, how to determine the right soil to cultivate vegetables, and how to improve the soil texture to produce maximum yields. You will also learn how to add fertilizers based on the soil pH value and increase soil concentration.

As a farmer, you may face several challenges like pest infection and diseases. In this guide, you we will go over how to manage and control pests in the greenhouse. This book will teach you how to know your crops are infected, about the various signs of different diseases, about the causes of these diseases, and how to prevent the spread of those diseases in your garden.

CHAPTER ONE

GREENHOUSE GARDENING

A **greenhouse** is a high-tech production facility or structure with a transparent roof material, like glass. The structure is suitable for growing seasonal plants or vegetables under regulated, climatic conditions.

If you're looking forward to growing fresh vegetables, fruits, and exotic herbs that can't survive under normal, seasonal conditions, then a greenhouse is the way to go. You can set up a greenhouse structure in your backyard to provide you with warm and stable environment for growing seasonal plants.

A greenhouse technology will protect your plants from harsh climatic conditions like wind, high temperatures, cold, extreme radiation, insects, and many plant diseases. The structure you build will provide fully controlled environmental conditions, making them ideal for product growth.

There are various types of greenhouses made with different designs and styles to consider when planning to set up a greenhouse. Depending on your needs and budget, you can choose one of the following greenhouse forms, under glass or a polycarbonate structure, to start gardening with.

Why Cultivate in a Greenhouse

Greenhouses offer a lot of advantages to the owner and provide you with an ideal environment to extend your growing season. Some advantages you will gain through installing a greenhouse in your backyard include:

Having a longer growing season: A greenhouse can extend the growing season and allow you to plant all-year round vegetables in a controlled environment. It also gives you the freedom to plant crops at the beginning or at the end of the season.

Control climate conditions: A greenhouse protects your crops from harsh weather conditions. The structure provide shield to your crops from extreme temperatures, strong winds, and even frost. You can install temperature and heating control tools inside the structure to regulate the climate, and you can also install lighting equipment and vents for constant air circulation.

Grow a variety of plants: Greenhouses give you the opportunity to grow a wide variety of crops. If there are certain plants that don't do well in your location, which you can plant in your greenhouse. You can adjust the greenhouse conditions to meet the growing requirements of the plant.

Pest control: Growing vegetables, herbs, and fruits in a shielded area is one of the most effective methods in controlling pests from infecting your plants. The closed structure prevents pests and other insects from attacking the plants, required that you come up with the right preventive measures.

Fresh produce: You will be able to harvest fresh vegetables, fruits, and herbs from your garden at anytime, whenever you need them.

Where to Start

Before buying or building your greenhouse, you need to determine how much space you need to grow your products and whether you need a *domestic* or *commercial* greenhouse. A greenhouse is a long-term investment; therefore, you need to be careful when making your selection for growing space. The space should be large enough to accommodate more plants in future, for example, if you want to plant vegetables or fruits, you need plenty of headroom and light.

You also need to do a research on the climate conditions, temperature, and moisture that would be suitable for growing your fruits, vegetables, and herbs of choice. This step is essential for the survival of your plants.

You need to plan for your planting schedule. A good plan should ensure you have constant supply of fruits and vegetables for all four seasons.

Greenhouses come in different styles that you can fit with several technological tools aimed at optimizing favorable climatic conditions for plant growth. Commercial greenhouses have computer-controlled equipment for cooling, heating, and lighting the structure. Different types of budget-friendly structures are available in the market, and you can build some of these structures within a day.

Site Selection for the Greenhouse

Before selecting the type of greenhouse, you need to look at the following requirements for your vegetables, herbs, and fruit garden. These factors can apply to other farmers dealing with other types of specialized crops. The requirements are also important when planning to expand your greenhouse in the future.

Quality water: The type of crops grown, type of irrigation system, and other factors like the climate of the area determine the amount of water you need in your greenhouse. You should also carry out a test to determine the water quality in the area like the pH level, hardness, electrical conductivity, alkalinity, and any other dissolved elements in the water. Ensure you have constant supply of water within the area; generally, the total daily consumption per square foot should be 0.3 gallons.

Adequate land: You need at least two acres of land for the greenhouse, parking area, buffers, and any other facility needed in the area. An extra vacant land in the area is essential for expansion of your garden once the business grows. The land should have an excellent soil type for providing drainage.

Topography of the area: Greenhouses are always built facing south; therefore, when choosing the site location, you should look for the one with a gentle slope facing the south. This is great for harness solar energy and providing adequate lighting inside the greenhouse. A site with at least 1% to 2% slope will help you cut down costs on the preparation of the site.

Site orientation: The selected site should have great access to solar all day. This ensures you capture enough light energy for the process of photosynthesis. The site should also have shelter belts (trees and shrubs) at least to the north side to protect your crops from harsh weather like strong wind. Shelter belts not only protect the crops but can also help in energy conservation.

Accessibility: The area selected should be easily accessible by road. Setting up the greenhouse on a highway will ensure there is fast delivery of your produce. If it's on a busy road, there is a high chance for your business growth due to increased customer base.

Other utilities: You need to consider other utilities like electricity and telephone system, and the cost of electricity and telephones services should be reasonable. Determining the cost of electricity all includes the operations, installation process, fuel consumption, and greenhouse type.

Rules and regulations: Before running any greenhouse, you need to get approval from the Federal, state, and local governments. You should also check building and wetlands regulations and get a license to operate the greenhouse. Different regulations apply to different countries, so make sure to do enough research based on the laws for that country.

Types of Greenhouses

The type of greenhouse structure determines the productivity and efficiency of your gardening activities. New to greenhouse gardening? Don't you worry—this section will examine the different greenhouse designs and highlight the advantages and disadvantages of each structure. It will make it easier for beginners to choose the right structure based on their needs.

As a plant grower, you need to understand the efficiency of plant production and control of environmental conditions. Choosing the right greenhouse will enable you to create an ideal working environment for your vegetables, herbs, and fruits. It also allows you to create a plant growing plan that ensures you meet the specific needs of your crop.

These designs are based on the materials, shape, utility, and construction process. Most designs are classified as:

Attached

- Lean-to greenhouse structure
- Even span greenhouse structure

Freestanding or independent structures

- Uneven span greenhouse structure
- A-frame greenhouse structure
- Quonset greenhouse structure
- Gothic arch greenhouse structure

Gutter connected structures

- Ridge and furrow type greenhouse
- Sawtooth greenhouse

Lean-to Greenhouse Structure

Just like the name suggests, a lean-to greenhouse structure is built leaning on the side of another structure. It is classified as an **attached greenhouse structure**, meaning that the roof of the greenhouse connects to another building. You don't have to build all the four walls of the greenhouse because, by design, it shares one of its walls.

Lean-to greenhouse structure

The structure should face the right direction to obtain adequate sunlight exposure. It should mostly face the southern side and the roof should have the best covering material. a lean-to greenhouse is ideal for growing herbs and vegetables.

GREENHOUSE

This structure was common during the Victorian period, and it is one of the *traditional* structures available. Building against the wall offers additional support to the structure, making it strong and wind resistant. The wall also absorbs heat during the day and releases that heat at night, which helps to maintain the temperature of the greenhouse during the cool nights.

If you're planning to use lean-to structure, you need to put the height of the structure into consideration together with any metal base. This ensures the ridges do not come in contact with any windows or drainage pipes in the principal building.

Advantages

- *Cost-effective*: This type of structure is less expensive compared to other greenhouse structures.
- *Minimize building materials*: The design is built against an existing wall, thus saving you on building material for four walls. It also minimizes roofing material requirements, since the design makes the best use of sunlight.
- The structure is constructed close to water, electricity, and heat.

Disadvantages

- *Limited sunlight*: Building lean-to structure against a house or garage limits the amount of sunlight to only the three walls. It will also have limited light, ventilation, and minimum temperature control.

- *Limited to the building orientation*: The best structure should be on the southern exposure. The height of the building or the supporting wall affects the design and the size of the greenhouse.

- *Temperature control*: It is difficult to control the temperature of the structure because the wall absorbs a lot of heat during the day and distributes it for use in the cool nights. Some translucent covers lose heat more rapidly, making it difficult to control the heat.

- *Foundation*: You need to build a strong foundation for this greenhouse to last long, especially when using glass with the lean-to greenhouse.

Even Span Greenhouse Structure

GREENHOUSE

Even span is another attached type of greenhouse, and it attaches more to promote plant growth. This standard structure is attached to a building, and its roof is made of two slopes of equal length and width. The structure can allow you to plant two to three rows, with two side benches and a wide bench at the center.

Even span design is more flexible and has curved eaves to boost their shape. Due to its great shape, there is plenty of air circulation in the greenhouse, thus making it easier to control temperatures. You also need to have an extra heating system especially when the structure is far away from a heated building. The heating system is especially important during the winter season.

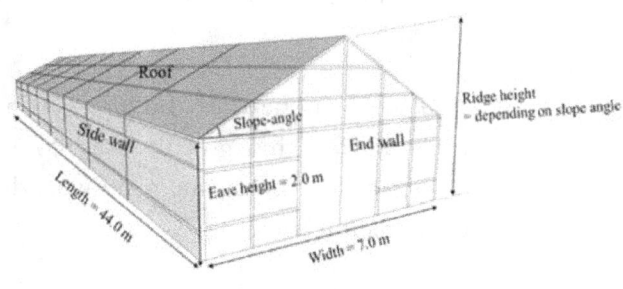

even span greenhouse structure

photo credit: researchgate.net

Advantages

- It provides enough space for the growth of plants and vegetables.

- It is easier and more economic in construction, making it the most popular design for a greenhouse.

- You have easy access to water and electricity within the building.

Disadvantages

- High cost of construction and heating system compared to the lean-to structure.

- Reduced sunlight exposure due to the shadow from the house it is attached to.

Uneven Span Greenhouse Structure

In this structure, the roof is made of uneven or unequal width. The greenhouse is constructed such that one rooftop slope is longer than the other, making the design suitable for a hilly terrain or when you want to take advantage of solar energy.

GREENHOUSE

Uneven slopes are laid so the steeper angles of the greenhouse face to the south. The transparent section should face south, whereas the opaque side of the greenhouse should face north to conserve energy.

Uneven greenhouses are no longer used because most farmers prefer setting up a greenhouse on a flat land.

Uneven-span greenhouse structure
Photo credit pinterest

Advantages

- As mentioned, this greenhouse is in a hilly areas.

- There is no obstruction of sunlight because the longer slope allows for more sunlight to enter the structure. The longer side also faces south, thus maximizing heat from the sun's rays.

Disadvantages

- It can be costly compared to even span greenhouses.

- They require more support on the slanted roof.

- Uneven span greenhouses usually need a lot of maintenance on the roof after some time.

- Too much solar can penetrate to the greenhouse if the uneven-span greenhouse is located in areas close to the equator.

A-Frame Greenhouse Structure

The A-frame greenhouse style is one of the most common designs. The structure is simple to set and it is ideal for a small backyard garden. To form the A-frame, you would attach the roof and sidewalls of greenhouse together, which forms a triangular-like shape.

Most of A-framed greenhouses use translucent, poly-carbonate material, which helps to eliminate the cost from having to buy glass material. Most A-framed greenhouses are laid down in an open field or at the backyard facing the southern side.

Advantages

GREENHOUSE

- It maximizes on the use of space along the side walls.

- Simple and straightforward to construct.

- Conservative structure style, using minimal material.

Disadvantages

- It has poor air circulation at the corners of the triangle.

- Its narrow side walls limit the overall use of the greenhouse.

Quonset Greenhouse Structure/ Hoop-House Structure

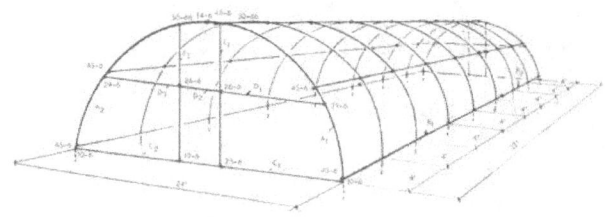

The quonset design has a curved roof or arched rafters, and its design is similar to military-hut style. The circular band in the structure's style is made of aluminum or PVC pipes, while the rooftop is made of plastic sheeting. The sidewalls of the design are set low, however, so there is not a whole lot of headroom. The hoops on the rooftop ensure there is no accumulation of snow and water on the top.

You would build this type of greenhouse in an open field or backyard with the structure facing the southern side.

Advantages

- Easy to build and one of the cheapest designs due to the use of plastic sheeting.

- Its design allows rain water and melted snow to run off.

- Suitable for a small plant growing space.

Disadvantages

- Limited storage space.

- Its frame design is not as sturdy as A-frame design.

GREENHOUSE

- As stated, there is less headroom in the structure.

Gothic Arch Greenhouse Structure

Gothic arch has a nice aesthetic, and is one of the most visually pleasing designs available. The walls of the structure are bent over a frame, forming a pointed roof-like structure. The design requires less material to construct, as there is no need for trusses. Most of Gothic arch designs are made of plastic sheeting, and its design allows you to construct a large greenhouse where you can plant various products in rows.

GREENHOUSE

Advantages

- The design has minimum heat exposure, thus making it easy to conserve heat.

- Plastic sheeting reduces the cost of construction.

- It has a simple and efficient design that allows rainwater and snow to flow away.

-

Disadvantages

- Not enough headroom and the design has a low sidewall height, which limits the storage of the greenhouse design.

Ridge and Furrow Greenhouse Structure

This type of design uses two or more A-framed design structures connected to one another along the roof eave length. The eaves offer more protection and act as a furrow to allow melted snow or rain water to flow away.

There are no side walls on the structure, which creates more ventilation in the greenhouse. It also reduces automation cost and fuel consumption, since only small wall area is exposed where the heat can escape.

Ridge and furrow greenhouse structure is ideal for growing vegetables, and they're mostly used in

GREENHOUSE

Europe, Canada, the Netherlands, and Scandinavian countries.

Advantages

- Ideal for large scale farming, and it's easy to expand this type of greenhouse.
- Provides more ventilation into the greenhouse.
- Requires few materials for construction because of its lack of side walls.
- Requires little energy to cool and heat.

Disadvantages

- Lack of proper water drainage system will damage your plants.
- Although the design has no side walls, shadows from the gutters can prevent sunlight from entering the greenhouse.

GREENHOUSE

Sawtooth Greenhouse Structure

This type of greenhouse structure is similar to the ridge and furrow; however, sawtooth offers more natural ventilation. This is due to its natural ventilation flow path developed as a result of the sawtooth design. The roof provides 25% of the total ventilation to the greenhouse, and opening the sawtooth vents will ensure there is continuous airflow into the greenhouse. This makes it easy to control the temperatures and ensure the plants are in good climatic conditions for their growth.

Advantages

GREENHOUSE

- Sawtooth arches provide excellent light transmission into the greenhouse.

- High rooftop allows for natural heat ventilation and airflow in the greenhouse.

- Excellent structure for both warm and cold climatic conditions.

- Simple and strong greenhouse structure.

- Has a large farming area.

Cold Frame Greenhouse Structure

Cold frame is ideal for greenhouse gardening in your backyard, and allows you to plant plants and vegetables at any time. It is one of the cheapest and simplest greenhouses you can set up. In cold frame gardening, you place a glass or plastic sheeting as the cover of the greenhouse structure, which will help in protecting your crops from frost, snow, rain, wind, or low temperatures.

Cold-frame greenhouse is suitable for planting cold-loving plants like broccoli, cauliflower, and cabbage among others.

Based on your budget, you can go for glass, polycarbonate, or plastic sheeting material to construct the greenhouse. The design requires a few openings to allow ventilation of heat into the greenhouse.

Advantages

- Simple design and easy to manage.
- Made from old windows or old wood pallets, which minimizes the cost of construction.

Disadvantages

- Overheating problem—a single day with a lot of sun and closed windows can do a lot of damage to the plants.

- Recycling of the old materials can affect the material quality of the greenhouse.

Hotbed Greenhouse

The hotbed structure acts as a miniature type of greenhouse that traps heat from solar radiation. This greenhouse can provide a favorable environment for plants that need a lot of heat like tomatoes, eggplants, and peppers.

If you want to extend the growing season, you can use hotbeds to provide the right weather conditions for your crops. Whether during winter, summer, or spring, there is always a family of vegetables, fruits, or herbs you can grow.

The hotbed structure provides a heat source to the crops through manure rather than using heat source from electricity, helping to speed up the growth of your plants.

When using a hotbed, you can set up the garden as wide as you want, provided the ratio of manure used and the growing medium is 3:1. The amount of time and money you invest in the garden will determine your farm produce success.

Advantages

- Simple to design.
- Inexpensive.

Disadvantages

- Hotbeds only lasts two months, so you will need to remove and replace the material with new ones around that time.

Window Farm

A window farm is an indoor farming garden for most vegetables. In a window farm, plants rely on the natural light from the window and temperature control from your living area to grow. This method is ideal for those who don't have a backyard or enough space to construct a standalone greenhouse.

You should set the structure in a window where it can receive a lot of light, facing toward the south.

Advantages

- Amazing for growing vegetables.
- Simple design and easy to construct.

Disadvantages

- Requires more components like nutrients, tubes, and pumps to grow your vegetables.

- It is difficult to maintain compared to a normal, soil-based greenhouse.

Construction of the Greenhouse

When building a greenhouse, you have to pay close attention to its base. Ensure you have a secure base and that it's leveled up. Most structures have a metal base designed from a metal frame, which is separate from the rest of the structure.

You need to secure the base on the ground to avoid any movement. Make sure it's strong enough to withstand heavy winds, as such an event could be disastrous.

Site planning for where to layout the greenhouse is important too, and you should also evaluate the soil. Depending on the soil underneath, you can prepare your soil structure and texture. For example, if the soil is light and sandy, you have to install concrete or use slabs in the area.

GREENHOUSE

Types of Greenhouse Foundations

Soil/Earth Base

If the selected site has firm soil, construct concrete walls at the four corners of the frame. Level up the base of the structure before setting in the concrete walls. If the area has a slope, you need to use more soil to level up and firmly compact it down using rollers or with a vibrating plate.

Creating a soil base greenhouse allows you to cultivate fruits and vegetables directly in the soil. You can also be assured of good drainage. A soil base greenhouse foundation is one of the cheapest methods for constructing a greenhouse; although, there is a possibility of the frames subsiding, leading the breakage on the glass material.

If the soil drains poorly, the greenhouse can become muddy and waterlogged, which can allow for rodents and pests to breed inside.

Perimeter Base

You can create a perimeter base for the greenhouse, which you can make from slabs, concrete material, or breeze blocks. Measure the size of the base, then mark it with spray paint. Firmly fix the slabs or blocks down with a mixture of cement.

GREENHOUSE

You can dig the area you want to fix to ensure you have a strong foundation. Laying the base directly on the sand can make the greenhouse unstable.

This kind of base provides you with a solid and cost-effective structure for building the greenhouse.

Slabs or Paving Base

If you're looking for aesthetic, then you should use a slabs base. Having this type of base makes it easy to maintain the greenhouse, and you can plant your vegetables and fruits on the growing bags, containers, or pots.

This type of base is long-lasting and firmly fixed on the ground with the use of heavy duty plugs and multiple screws.

You can easily reorganize your greenhouse and keep it clean with this base. Water will be able to drain easily via the cracks on the slabs, though growing plants will be limited to using growing pots, bags, and containers.

It is the most expensive compared to perimeter and soil base.

Concrete Base

A concrete base is suitable if you plan to build a large greenhouse, as it makes it easy to raise the base level. Concrete base has a durable foundation and you can easily clean the base using a detergent soap and water, or by simply sweeping the area with a broom. Washing this base with detergents can also help keep diseases away from the greenhouse.

Make sure to drill holes on the concrete to allow proper drainage of water in the greenhouse.

Once you have the base set up, you can construct the type of greenhouse style and start growing your plants.

Layout of the Greenhouse Site

Using what you now know about the various greenhouse styles, you can choose the right one based on your needs and come up with the site layout for your garden. Follow through this guide to know how to set up a layout for your garden.

Set-up greenhouse plan: You need to come up with a master plan for constructing buildings or facilities within the site. The plan should show detailed information on existing facilities within the site, evaluate any constraints and benefits of the site, and determine where to construct a new facility.

A good plan will outline where to construct the greenhouse, where to build a storage area, and the headhouse. If you're planning to have an outdoor production, then the area you select should be only a few meters away, which will make shipping and moving the crops easier.

A headhouse is building that attaches to the greenhouse, or is a converted section in the greenhouse that acts as a working area, office, utility room, or a transplanting area.

You should plan for the expansion space. You can start out small at first, but as your business grows, you may want to expand the greenhouse; therefore, it is important to factor in expansion space in your master plan. Once you are satisfied with the plan, you can go ahead and look at other factors.

Parking area and access to facilities: If you're setting up a commercial greenhouse facility, you need to ensure employees can conveniently access the growing area by providing a good parking area. Ensure the site has enough parking space for loading vehicles within the storage buildings and growing area, and employees and customers should also have their own parking lot. You will need to build all driveways and parking areas sloping to provide proper drainage.

Alternatively, you can use underground piping to carry the water away.

Storage area: An indoor storage area is essential to store the harvested crops before shipping and transportation to the retail market. You also need a storage area for all farm equipment, containers, and chemicals, which can either be a separate building or in a headhouse. An outdoor storage area can be used for growing mix.

Outdoor facilities: You can set up an outdoor production facility to act as the growing bed or a shade house. The structure should have adequate lighting, a good drainage system, and an adequate water supply. The production area should be in a rectangular shape measuring about 1000 to 2000 square feet.

Chapter Summary

The key to successful gardening is meeting all the requirements for your garden. You also have to come up with site layout that will guide you in planning all your gardening facilities. Greenhouse gardening can help you maximize your crop production. A well-designed greenhouse will ensure there is maximum space utilization and enable you to accurately control temperature conditions.

The right greenhouse structure is one that will last you a long time. Choose a design that meets your demands and fits in your budget. Once satisfied with a particular type of greenhouse design, you should learn more on how to utilize the greenhouse to grow the best produce.

The foundation of the structure chosen also contributes to the success of the greenhouse. Choosing a long-lasting base structure will help you set up a strong greenhouse structure with less maintenance. The base structure will determine the drainage system in the area and help you better understand the soil you need in your garden.

Growing vegetables or herbs in the greenhouse allows you to control the climate conditions within the growing environment and any other external constraints. To yield maximum benefit, you need a tailor-made greenhouse that helps you increase produce for your vegetables, fruits, and herbs. Always remember that what has worked for someone else may not work for you or meet your own requirements; therefore, you should start small and grow your garden with time.

In the next chapter, you will learn how various climatic conditions may affect your greenhouse garden.

CHAPTER TWO

OPERATING A GREENHOUSE

Growing the plants in the greenhouse can be your ultimate dream; however, there is more to greenhouse than just setting up the structure. You need to know how to maintain the greenhouse and ensure there is optimum conditions for the plants to thrive.

Having your own greenhouse will enable you to grow vegetables all year round, exotic plants, or herbs, and start the seeding process early. There are many reasons why you should set up your own greenhouse garden.

From the previous chapter, you learned that greenhouses come in a variety of styles and designs, ranging from a simple framed structure to full-size glass construction. Depending on your needs, you can purchase or build your own structure.

Each greenhouse model includes some temperature control features and other components to help you utilize the greenhouse's functions. Some of these components or amenities include electricity, heat, water, lighting, shelves, and benches. For example, the heating system enables you to grow your plants anytime of the year, so you don't have to worry about which season is the best for growing each crop. The lighting will enable you walk into the garden, even in the dark, and work on the crops, including planting new ones, trimming, and cutting.

Controlling Temperature Conditions

Controlling the temperatures within the greenhouse is essential for your crops' survival. Let's look at each of the following conditions and how you can regulate them and maximize on your produce.

Heating

Once you set up the greenhouse, you need to keep the temperature of greenhouse between 80° to 85°F (27° to 29°C). During the day, the greenhouse harnesses heat energy from the sun's rays and uses it to heat the internal air inside the garden. You can also get heat from other sources like electric heaters or gas.

A hot water boiler is highly recommended as a heating system. Water temperature should be regulated to satisfy the needs of each heating system. Depending on the specific crop's needs, each greenhouse should have independent temperature control.

Any of these heat sources can quickly heat up the structure to higher temperatures of over 100°F (40°C), which can kill your crops. Therefore, you need to regulate the interior temperature to a range of 80° to 85°F (27° to 30°C).

Ventilation and Air Flow

When designing a greenhouse, you must include vents either at the rooftop that with a hatch you can open on the ceiling, or have side vents. Plants need carbon dioxide (CO_2) to grow and release oxygen (O_2)

and moisture into the environment. You need good ventilation in the area to avoid growing the crops under humid conditions.

Fans will be a great addition for cooling the environment, as they can whisk out the hot air and introduce a cooler air inside. You can choose to operate the vents either manually or automatically. If you install manual vents, make sure you open them every day and close them at night.

If you're on a budget, the manual vent system can work for you as long as you will always be available to open and close it as the weather changes. If you're not always around, maintaining a manual vent system may be difficult for you; therefore, an automated system would be the best alternative.

GREENHOUSE

An automatic ventilation system uses a sensor programmed to automatically turn on the fans or the heating system when temperatures change. The sensors monitor temperatures when they rise and fall and automatically switch the fans and heaters on or off. This ensures constant air circulation and cooling of the greenhouse structure.

During the warmer days, you can ensure there is enough ventilation by opening the door to your garden. Make sure to put a heavy rock on the door or tie it to prevent wind from shutting it. If the structure is made of cold frames, you can also open the lid to allow more air to circulate inside during the day.

Lighting

To control the light levels, you need to have a shade cloth in either green or any other dark color. You can place the material on all the windows on the outside of the greenhouse, and you can roll it up and down to adjust the temperatures inside the greenhouse. This material will act as a shade and can prevent an excess of light from entering through the windows.

The shade cloth is crucial during the summer months. It helps in regulating heat and cooling the greenhouse temperatures, while allowing moderate light inside the structure. During the winter months, you can roll the cloth up to allow more light to enter inside.

Humidity

The amount of humidity present in your garden is essential in determining your vegetables' survival. You must keep the garden environment humid at all times, and at least ensure you have a humidity of 50% or higher.

The best strategies for adding more humidity to your crops is through:

- Taking a tray of pebbles and placing it under your crops.

- Covering the pebbles with water and putting them near the crops. As the water in the pebbles evaporates, it adds more humidity in the air.

- Placing stone chips or marbles under the crop benches or on a table. These stone chips may add more humidity to the crops, especially when placed on a dry day.

Benches are great for keeping moisture away. A **bench** is a type of table that has lips at the edge, and it is used to hold plants in place. Wooden benches have a tray inserted on it to keep moisture away from the wood, whereas metal benches have a mesh top attached to them to make it easy drain water and moisture.

How to Keep the Greenhouse Warm

1. Using Bubble Wrap to Insulate the Greenhouse

Insulating a greenhouse garden with a bubble wrap will ensure heat doesn't escape away. For a better insulation, buy a wrap with bigger bubbles. You should also cover all doors and windows to ensure heat doesn't escape, especially during the winter. This practice will not only keep the greenhouse warm, but it will also reduce the cost of heating.

2. Using Heaters

A small heater added to the greenhouse can help regulate the greenhouse's temperature, especially during the night. The plants can use the carbon dioxide produced by the heater and convert it to oxygen, which is essential for humans.

The cold weather outside will not be able to affect your plants inside the greenhouse if you have a heater installed.

3. Using Air Circulators Inside the Greenhouse

Heaters will not be enough to provide warmth inside the greenhouse; you will also have to make sure the fresh air being circulated inside the greenhouse is warmed evenly to avoid having cold and hot patches on the plants.

Installing air circulators will ensure there is an even distribution of warm air inside the greenhouse. You can buy an air circulator fan or use the air circulation function from KlimaHeat to mix air.

If you have no electricity in the area, you can protect the plants from the cold weather by:

1. Using Compost

The bacteria that breaks down organic matter during the compost process generates heat; therefore, adding more compost to the soil will help generate heat that can keep your plants warm.

Add a layer of soil about 3 inches thick to enable the bacteria to create a warm environment for the plant roots.

2. Using a Double Layer of Plastic Material to Make Windows

Insulating the windows can help the greenhouse retain more heat. Although insulation can block the amount of light from entering, using a double layer of insulation material on the windows can add more warmth inside. As a result, you double the R-value (insulation) of the greenhouse.

3. Using Black Mulch on All Pathways

The pathways inside the greenhouse or between the planting beds absorb heat. Adding black mulch, or any other dark color mulch, to the pathways will absorb more sunlight and convert it to heat, keeping your plants' roots warm.

4. Using Heat to Absorb Barrels

Put black barrels in an area where they can have direct access to sunlight, as they will absorb more sunlight and use that to convert heat that will warm the water inside. As it goes, you should place the plastic black barrels in water.

The warm water created will act as thermal mass and can hold for a longer period, providing warmth to greenhouse plants.

Although they use sunlight themselves, make sure to place the barrels in a way that they won't block sunlight from reaching the plants. Barrels work well when placed on the northern corner of the greenhouse. During the summer, you should cover these barrels with a white material to prevent them from creating extra heat in the greenhouse.

5. Building the Greenhouse Partially Underground

Building the greenhouse 4 inches deeper on the ground will help retain more warmth and acts as an insulator against the cold air from outside the structure. During the cold season, the ground will be warm. This provides the warmth needed for the roots of the plant to grow.

If you have a greenhouse building facing the south hillside, it will absorb more heat to warm the ground.

6. Utilizing Thermal Mass Objects

Using objects like clay, rocks, and bricks can absorb heat when the air circulating inside is warm and release the absorbed heat when the air inside is cold. Therefore, having raised beds made of clay or brick material can absorb heat and use it to warm the greenhouse. You can boost the amount of warmth released by adding black barrel to water inside.

7. Insulating the Northern Side

If you stay in Northern hemisphere, there is no need to fix glass on the northern side because the sun doesn't shine on that side. Adding insulators on the northern side will help retain heat inside the greenhouse and prevent north winds from getting inside. In addition, putting a thermal heating mass on the wall can absorb more sunlight.

GREENHOUSE

Chapter Summary

Greenhouses need to be set to optimum conditions for the plants to thrive. Building your own greenhouse allows you to adjust climatic condition to match the one suitable for the growth of plants and extend the growing season, meaning you won't have to stick to growing plants during the warm weather. Using a greenhouse, you can grow all-year round plants and have a constant supply of fresh food from your firm.

Both fruits, vegetables, and herbs require different climatic conditions, and depending on your location, you can adjust greenhouse temperatures, lighting, and humidity to match your crop needs.

You have to install vents and fans in the greenhouse to ensure there is fresh air circulation in the structure and make the conditions unfavorable for breeding of pests and diseases.

To maximize the plants' yields, you need to maintain a good growing environment and ensure the greenhouse is kept warm at all times. There are various tools you can use to ensure the greenhouse stays warm or utilize non-electrical methods to keep the structure warm.

In the next chapter, you will learn about various tools and equipment essential for running a greenhouse.

CHAPTER THREE

GREENHOUSE EQUIPMENT

Having the best greenhouse equipment is crucial for efficiently managing your greenhouse. The equipment will help in your operation, maintenance, and improvement of the greenhouse, and there is a wide variety of equipment and other accessories for all your greenhouse in the market.

The choice of equipment to use depends on the types of crops and the climatic conditions of the area. That is, are you located in an area that experience heavy snow and with a lot of wind, or are you in an area that experiences extreme heat or cold? This information is important when buying greenhouse equipment.

The equipment used only for raising seedling will be different to those you would use for full cycle planting fruits or vegetables. Your choice of the equipment and other accessories will ensure your ability to produce high quality crops and maintain an active produce for all-year round crops. You should keep the greenhouse structure warm and properly managed to create more space for plant germination.

Depending on the type of crop, planting can be on the floor or on the benches. A fixed peninsula and movable benches are highly recommended, as they help in creating more growing space. Other equipment like overhead conveyor trolleys and carts can contribute to reduced cost of material handling.

Basic Equipment

When you think of starting your own greenhouse garden, there are basic considerations you need to think about, such as where to get the seeds, pots, and trays to plant your crops.

The choice of these greenhouse containers will have an impact on how the vegetables, herbs, and the fruits grow.

The containers you use in the garden should be able to grip the soil and promote good health to the seeds. They should also offer enough room for the roots to grow and provide an excellent drainage system. This ensures the crops are in good condition and promote their growth.

Containers can hold several planting trays and pots to provide crop growth and stability, and as a result, there will be an upward growth to your crops. These containers can be in the form of plugs, flats, pots, and hanging baskets. A larger container can fit several pots inside and provide enough space to grow the seeds.

Hanging baskets are great for planting your vegetables and herbs in the garden. There are plenty of these baskets in the market, and they will provide enough space for your crops' growth. Most of the baskets will be plastic or coconut fiber, while others will be made of ceramic metal. You can buy any material based on your budget.

You would use **flats** and **plugs** during the *germination stage*. They ensure the vegetables grow separately and keep your garden neat.

Most gardeners prefer pots made of **clay**, as they give the growing of plants like fruits, flowers, and vegetables a more traditional look. If you're on a budget, you can buy **plastic pots** or **wood pots**, which are more durable and cheaper. You can dispose of plastic and wood pots much easier than clay pots.

You can also consider the use of seed boxes to help you in the germination of the seeds. The boxes can be made of plastic or wood material and they provide you with excellent space to grow your fruits and vegetables.

How to Choose Good Containers and Pots

If you're using **porous containers**, you will find that you have to continue watering the crops, as the soil dries out very quickly. This can lead to wasting water and increase the cost of water. In **non-porous containers**, you use less water because the soil grips moisture, thus, retaining enough water content for a day.

Therefore, when choosing any of those containers discussed above, they should not only satisfy the growth of crops but also provide enough drainage and porosity.

Mobility of the pots and containers is also important, especially if plan to have all-year-round crops in the garden. They should be made of lightweight material to make it easy to move them around.

Choosing the right container will contribute significantly to the growth of vegetables, herbs, and fruits in your greenhouse.

Furniture to Store Greenhouse Equipment

Shelves: You need a furniture that will help you arrange all the containers and provide adequate **shelving** in the greenhouse. If you have a small space in the greenhouse, you can use shelves to boost on the growing space.

There are movable greenhouse shelves that you can move out and back inside during favorable climatic conditions.

Always remember that **double shelving** can affect the amount of lighting required by the crops.

You can build temporary shelves or have permanent shelves attached to the structure to start your seedlings. You can also have shelves built beneath the garden benches to help you create more space in the greenhouse.

You can build shelves made of wood, glass, or metal. The wire mesh you use in building the shelves helps in draining the excess water from the crops.

Another important reason for creating shelves is to ensure all the crops are separate from one another to avoid **cross-pollination**. Depending on the size of the shelves, it can store more pots and containers.

Garden benches: Another furniture inside the greenhouse are **garden benches**. The greenhouse structure determines the size of the benches in the garden, and these benches can be temporary or permanently built. Installing benches is great for optimizing the growing space in the garden, and section benches are ideal for regular movement and creating new plant arrangements.

Planters: These are widely common in today's modern greenhouse gardens. The long and deep **planters** are highly recommended for growing fruits, vegetables, or any other food crops. The planters are designed in such a way that each can only hold a single vegetable or fruit plant.

Lighting System Equipment

The amount of light inside the greenhouse determines the level of sunlight in the greenhouse. If the amount of sunlight in the greenhouse is not strong enough, you can supplement it with artificial light.

Before choosing the lighting system to use for boosting plant growth, you need to determine the amount of solar radiation available in that area, as that will affect the amount of light needed for photosynthesis.

Others factors you need to look at is the size and type of greenhouse structure. You also need to consider the crops growing, as some of them require high-intensity light, while others will do better in low light or shade.

You should consider the space available for hanging the lighting system, and it should be easy to adjust based on the crops' needs. For example, as some plants, like fruits, increase in height as they grow, the lighting system should be moved upwards. Therefore, you need to factor in the wiring system and the socket space.

Some of the tools for providing artificial light include:

Light intensity meter: This instrument has an installed universal-sensor probe that measures the intensity of light at any angle. The equipment monitor can maintain an ideal growing light for all plants in the garden.

Grow lights: Grow lights are excellent for providing a cool and warm light for the growth of house plants, herbs, and fruits. The grow lights act as a replacement of sunlight when growing plants indoors. There are different types of grow lights in the market to choose from, such as fluorescent, LEDs, high pressure sodium, among others.

Seedling lights: As the seeds germinate, they require a lot of light; therefore, you need to place them in an area where they can have a maximum access to light. Each plant grown requires a different light intensity, and most plants in a greenhouse garden require a high light intensity to flourish. You can have fluorescent bulbs installed in the garden to provide maximum light to all your crops.

High Intensity Discharge lamp (HID): If you have a large greenhouse structure with big plants like fruits and flowers, you need to install HID lamps. These lamps emit more light compared to other types of lights, boosting plant growth. The lamp fixtures have reflectors fitted on it to reflect the light back to the crops.

This type of lamp produces a lot of heat, so you should keep it far away from the plants to avoid burning their leaves.

LED Lights: LED lights are suitable for vegetables and herbs. They're the best greenhouse lights and the most efficient for quick plant growth. The lights are long-lasting and easy to install.

Temperature Control and Heating System Equipment

To control the temperature, you need to install an **electronic controller** in the garden. This control will monitor and manage the temperatures of the heating system and ventilation equipment.

Thermostats: If you have a small greenhouse garden, you can use thermostats that record accurate temperatures within the garden, and they automatically control the temperature in a specific area. Make sure it is installed based on the plant height as this will make it easy to capture accurate readings on temperature conditions.

Thermometer: A thermometer measures the maximum and minimum temperature inside the garden and monitors any temperature changes. It helps in maintaining perfect temperatures for the growth of plants.

When buying thermometer for the greenhouse, look for one that is reset by a magnet. Although there are other types, the one with a magnet is highly recommended for greenhouses.

Hot air furnace or unit heaters: The unit heater is suitable when the greenhouse is shutdown during the winter season to drain water system. Installing unit heaters is one of the best decisions you can make for your crop production, as they control the temperature inside the greenhouse.

There are different types of heaters and based on your garden needs, such as gas, electric, or propane.

GREENHOUSE

You can also choose to use **vented** on **non-vented** heaters.

EPDM tubing: Temperature control on the benches or floor is also important. You can place the EPDM tubing on the concrete floor or in a sand layer to provide floor heating. If you plant your crops on the benches, you can place the EPDM tubing on the bench or use a low output radiation pin, which you would place under the bench to keep the area warm.

Hot water boiler: A hot water boiler is the best for maintaining the heating system. Make sure the water temperatures don't go beyond 75°F (24°C). The root zone heat provides the uniform temperatures of 70°F to 75°F (21°C to 24°C), which is essential for all plant growth. Root zone heat provides 25% of the heat needed for the coldest nights, while the remaining 75% heat comes from heat exchangers or a radiation pin installed under the gutters or around the perimeter of the greenhouse.

Humidistat: A humidistat equipment is needed to control moisture or humidity within the greenhouse.

In a large scale operation, you can easily integrate computer controls in the ventilation, lighting, and heating systems. Using computer-controlled systems ensures automatic control of environmental conditions within the greenhouse.

Ventilation Equipment

A proper ventilation system contributes to the growth of your plants. Sunlight changes throughout the year can cause temperature changes in the garden, so you need to have a good venting system installed to control the temperatures.

Vents: You can install vents on the roof or on the sides of the structure. Rooftop vents are the most common and one of the best venting systems.

If you're not around throughout the day, an automatic venting system will be ideal for you.

Exhaust fans: You would use exhaust fans to whisk away excess air and ensure there is a constant supply of fresh air inside.

Water Management Equipment Irrigation Equipment

If you're using plug trays with small cells for growing the crops, then you should have a programmed computer irrigation system to water different section of crops at different rates. Automating the watering system will make your work easier.

GREENHOUSE

Customizing the watering system based on the individual needs of the crop bed ensures there is no overwatering or underwatering for each crop bed.

Plastic watering cans are highly recommended. They are cheap, lighter, and require less labor. However, if you want to maintain the beauty of the greenhouse, then you can use metal cans instead.

Another piece of equipment you can use is the **trickle watering system**. The trickle watering system uses a plastic horse with some outlet nozzles fitted at different intervals on the horse length.

You would place the horse pipes at proximity along the pots. Then, connect the horse to the water storage tank. You should fill the tanks with water consistently. Once full, it will release the water to all the crops.

The horse system will always water the pots and crop bed with a set water quantity and at the same time every day.

Other water equipment you will need in the garden include irrigation tubes, valves, water breakers, sprinklers, a hose, misters, and boilers. Boilers provide excellent temperature regulation.

Energy Conservation Equipment

GREENHOUSE

Due to the high cost of fuel energy, coming up with energy conservation measures will help you reduce the cost of production. Some essential tools for energy conservation include perimeter insulation, energy screens or shades, and windbreakers.

Pest Control Equipment

Every greenhouse structure should have a pest control system. There are different methods you can use to control pests in the farm, some of which use chemicals while others use biological methods.

You can also use natural methods, like beneficial insects, to control pests.

Alternatively, you can use a metal, cloth, or thin plastic mesh to keep pests away from the garden. Fencing and use of door sweeps can also keep the bugs away from accessing specific planting sections.

Depending on which method to use, you can buy sprayers, fogging equipment, and formers.

You can also use insecticide and pesticide to protect vegetables and keep attacking bugs at bay.

Other Greenhouse Accessories

Soil Sterilizer

Although you may be considering using any of the available types of soil for potting the vegetables, you can also consider the use of **soil fertilizers**. There are various methods you can use to sterilize the soil, but the best method is using a **steam sterilization system**.

Installing a steam system is easy and cheap and ensures efficiency in your gardening.

Gardening Sieves

The soil texture is an important factor you have to consider in the seedling stage. It is important to ensure that you use the best texture for your baby plants to survive. A **sowing sieve** will help you achieve your goal by providing you with the desired texture for the baby plants.

You can also use a mesh sieve, which lightly covers the seeds with a compost once you plant them.

Plant Supporting Equipment

GREENHOUSE

Sometimes, to increase your plants' strength and length, you can introduce the support equipment to provide adequate support to them as they grow. One way to provide support is by tying them together, so they can help hold each other up.

There are different materials you can use to tie the plants together, but you can try **raffia**, as it supports most of plants, and various stores sell it at a reasonable price.

To use raffia, you can soak it in water for a few hours before tying the plants with it. This practice helps avoid breakage and makes it stronger and more reliable.

Chapter Summary

You need to keep your greenhouses warm and properly arranged to create more space for plant germination. Depending on the type of crop, planting can be on the floor or on the benches. A fixed peninsula and movable benches are highly recommended, as they help to add more growing space. Other equipment like overhead conveyor trolleys and carts can contribute to reduced cost of material handling.

You also need to install temperature control equipment to monitor the room temperature and adjust it based on the crops' needs.

The plants growing area should be well-ventilated to ensure the garden is free from any moisture or humid conditions, and there should be enough lighting to quicken the plants' growth. If the greenhouse is set in an area where there is no direct access to sunlight, you can use artificial lighting equipment as a supplement.

Other basic tools like benches and containers for seedlings are crucial for plant survival. All plants, no matter the method of plantation, require a good drainage system.

You need to maintain proper hygiene on all tools and accessories used in the greenhouse, which will help

GREENHOUSE

keep diseases at bay. You should set up a storage room too, either within the greenhouse or in a separate building, where you can store all these tools.

In the next chapter, you will learn how to cultivate fruit.

CHAPTER FOUR

CULTIVATING FRUITS

Fruits are excellent, healthy snacks for people, and are great in foods too. The nutrient value of fruits can motivate us to become fruit farmers to supply fresh fruits to a large community. However, growing your own fruit at home can be limited to the prevailing climatic conditions within the environment, and sometimes, the weather patterns are not suitable for certain types of fruits. In certain areas where there is a short growing season, or an area that faces a lot of winter cold and frost, greenhouses will be ideal for growing fruit.

Greenhouse gardens allow you to cultivate all kinds of fruit trees and control the greenhouse temperatures to ensure you can get a healthy harvest. You can grow some fruits all year round inside the greenhouse, while others may require you to move the fruit tree inside during the winter season.

Whether you are setting up a home greenhouse or a commercial greenhouse, this tutorial will guide you on how to cultivate fruits.

GREENHOUSE

You can plant fruit trees, vines, or shrubs in containers or pots. During the seedling stage, you should grow the fruits at low humidity levels to enable them thrive. Doing this also protects the fruits from pests and other diseases.

Greenhouse gardening opens doors to fruit diversification by allowing you to cultivate different types of fruits and employ different farming styles and techniques.

Some fruits like lemons, peaches, grapes, strawberries, and tomatoes are less demanding. Grapes need a cool growing environment to thrive, as water-logged soil can affect their vines. Therefore, you will need free-draining soil cultivate the fruit.

Young fruit trees require support to grow strong, and you can tie the fruit trees together to support each other.

Based on the fruit you want to cultivate, you can control the greenhouse temperature, light, humidity, and other factors to satisfy your crops climatic needs and boost their growth.

Most fruit trees thrive well in temperatures above 50°F (10°C). Other tropical fruit-trees like citrus require a temperature of 60^0 F (16°C).

Getting Started With the Seedling Stage

To start, you need to add the moist seed-starting mix to all the pots and seed starting trays. Then, plant the seeds in the pots based on the directions given on the seeds' packets. Most seed supplier companies recommend planting two to three seeds per pot. Once you have planted them, use soil to cover the seeds and water them with a good amount of water. Cover the pot or the seedling containers with a plastic wrap and place them in a brightly lit environment to speed up the seed growth. You should also monitor the temperature in the room to ensure it is conducive for the fruits growth.

You can invest in an electric heating mat, which will help in regulating the soil temperatures for the seeds' starting stage. Once the seeds germinate, you should remove the plastic wrap.

You should keep the planting mix moist at all times. Do not overwater the mix, as doing so may affect the plants' growth.

Using scissors, snip out excess seeding in the pot or container. Each pot should only have **one fruit tree** to grow well.

Adding Fertilizers

You should fertilize the fruit plant after every one or two weeks to keep the fruit tree's health optimal. Water each pot with ¼ cup of water soluble fertilizer, and do so after adding fertilizers to them.

After eight weeks, the fruit tree is ready to be transplanted to a larger container to continue growing, or planted outside if the climate is favorable for that type of fruit.

Always ensure proper maintenance of the greenhouse. You should put moisture retention mechanisms and free soil drainage practices to produce tasty fruits.

Soil Preparation

Soil preparation is an essential part of producing healthy fruits. There is nothing more satisfying than harvesting fresh, tasty fruits from your own backyard, which is the dream of every farmer. To get better results for your produce, it all begins from the soil preparation and planning.

Soil preparation involves coming up with a way to improve the soil you used for planting the fruits. This practice requires improving the soil nutrients, its composition, pH balance, soil consistency, and drainage.

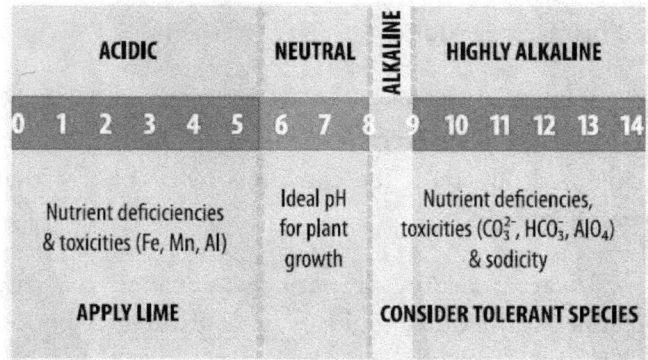

Proper preparation of the soil will ensure you harvest delicious and tasty fruits. The right type of soil should be able to increase the fruit production.

Fruit trees do well in soils with proper drainage and nutrients.

How to Improve Soil Drainage and Consistency

1. *Test Soil Drainage*

You can dig a hole in the planting area and fill it with water. The soil should be able to drain the water in three to four hours. Add more water and wait to drain it in three to four hours. If the water could not drain within that period, it is an indicator that the soil can't drain water enough and it *cannot* support the fruit tree's growth.

If it drains in less than three hours, the soil in that area is *sandy*. You can improve this by adding more organic matter into the soil.

You can improve soil drainage by building a drainage system, having raised beds in the greenhouse, or planting mounds.

2. Install a French Drainage System

If you're having a slow draining soil in the area, you can install French drains to speed up the drainage. Slow draining soil can be due to a thick and sticky clay layer clogging up underneath the topsoil. Installing the underground drainage pipes (French drainage system) can help solve the problem.

3. Use Organic Matter to Improve Soil Damage

If the soil is sandy and it rains quicker, the fruit trees may not get enough water to enable them grow healthy. You can solve this problem by adding a mix of composted organic matter to the soil. Doing this will help the soil to retain more moisture while the fruit tree roots are being established.

You can use a **rototiller** to mix the compost to the soil. You can buy or rent one from your local garden center.

After mixing the soil with organic matter, test it again with water and observe the drainage. As stated, it should drain within three to four hours.

The amount of organic matter added to the soil will depend on the rate of your soil drainage.

4. Protect the Tree Root Crown with a Mound

The root part of the fruit tree below the soil level is called the root crown. The **root crown** is vulnerable to excess moisture in the soil; therefore, you need to raise the planting area using a mound.

You can create a raised mound in your planting area by backfilling soil in the holes. This creates a gentle slope and raises the planting area, and the gentle slope prevents soil erosion.

5. Build a Raised Bed to Protect the Root Crown

You can also use raised beds instead to prevent soil erosion caused by the mounds.

You can build a raised bed through designing a simple wooden box, which will hold the soil around the fruit tree. The wooden box keeps the soil line raised high, and thus protecting the root crown from excess moisture.

6. Break Up the Soil Consistency for Better Root Growth

Tightly packed soil can limit the root growth. Fruit roots tend to do well in areas that are cultivated using shovels or rototiller, so you can use shovels to cultivate the planting area and break up the soil in that area.

Always make sure you don't cultivate below the recommended depth of planting fruit trees. If you notice the soil has a lot of clay as you cultivate, you can cut channels to create some holes. Doing this will prompt an outward root growth.

How to Test Soil Nutrients and pH

1. Use Soil Testing Kit

Nutrient soil testing kits are widely available. You can buy them from any hardware store or retailer like

Home Depot, Walmart, or Target. The kit comes in different forms, and all of which will work for your needs. They test the soil and give results on its nutrients and pH level.

You can also send soil samples to the lab for further analysis. Some kits also provide home and lab testing; however, they are more expensive compared to other home testing kits.

2. Test Soil During Early Summer

Although you can test the soil at any time, choosing to test the soil in early summer or late spring will give you enough time to make adjustments to the soil before the next planting season. If you are in an area with different planting season, you can carry out testing at either the start of the growing season or at the end of the previous growing season.

Also note that the presence of moisture in the soil can give incorrect readings, so early tests may be more ideal.

3. Clean the Testing Tools

Before taking any soil samples, you need to clean the tools using mild soap and water. Make sure to properly rinse the soap well; otherwise, you will get a wrong reading. Use a paper towel to dry the tools, then you can test the sample taken.

4. Take Soil Samples from the Planting Area

When taking the soil samples, dig some holes spaced evenly from the planting area and take samples from each hole to test. Put all the samples in a dry, clean bucket and mix them well. After mixing, you can put them on dry newspaper to let them dry.

You can use a sample container packed with the testing kit to ensure you take an equal amount of sample soil from each hole.

Once the soil sample is dry, add the reagent to the sample. As the soil reacts to the reagent, you should see the change in color, and you can read the result based on the pH level color chart provided in the kit.

How to Balance pH Level and Fertilize the Soil

From the provided pH level color chart, you can discern the type of soil you have, whether acidic or alkaline. Based on the results, you can decide to lower or increase the pH level, or whether to add more fertilizer to the soil to boost its nutrient value.

You can balance the pH by:

1. Reducing Soil Acidity

If the test shows the soil has high acidity, you need to reduce the excess acidity in the soil. One way of reducing the acidity level is to mix the soil with limestone. Make sure to follow the manufacturer's instructions for the quantity you should use for every mix.

You can add limestone each year at the beginning of every fall or during the summer. It may take some time before you can see the changes on the fruit's produce.

2. Increasing the pH Level

When the soil is alkaline, you can add some additives like sulfur or gypsum to increase its pH. You can also apply compost material to the soil regularly to reduce its alkalinity.

Make sure to always test the soil every time you add compost; otherwise, you may make the soil too acidic.

3. Fertilizing the Fruit Tree

Always add fertilizers to the fruit tree after planting. You should add the fertilizer at the top of the soil, mainly after the pruning process or before the budding of fruits.

Fruit roots are sensitive; therefore, you should avoid applying fertilizers or any manure directly to the hole where you will plant them.

4. *Adding Nitrogen Fertilizer on the Fruit Tree*

Once the fruit tree has grown to be strong, you can add nitrogen light fertilizer. However, this practice will reduce fruit bearing wood, and you will have to trim a lot of overgrown branches or stems to encourage fruit growth.

As mentioned, if the soil has a more acidic pH, you can add more lime to the soil to raise its pH and make it more suitable for planting fruits. If the soil pH is not acidic enough, you can use sulfur to lower it.

Each soil additive has a different pH concentration, so always follow the manufacturer's instructions in each additive to adjust the pH level to where you need it to be.

You may note that, in most areas, clay soil has more nutrients and poor drainage. In such cases, you don't need to add more fertilizer to the soil—you only need to use compost manure to improve the soil drainage.

If you are cultivating fruits for commercial use, you can use potted fruit trees in a potting soil. You can create potting soil mixture by mixing equal proportions of peat, sand, and bark or perlite, and the mixture you use should have proper drainage. To boost the pot drainage, you can use a pot with large drainage holes. You can also place a layer of gravel at the bottom of the pot.

Water Requirements for Planting Fruits

Fruit trees require plenty of water for it to produce juicy fruit. The more water it receives, the juicier it will be. A young fruit tree will need a lot of water for its growth, which is especially true during hot and dry periods.

If the fruit doesn't receive enough water up to its roots end, it will develop a weak fruit tree with a shallow root system. Giving the right amount of water to the fruit tree is essential for producing a decent amount of fruits.

Watering Baby Fruit Trees

A newly planted fruit tree requires a lot of water to establish strong roots in the soil. Watering the fruit tree with plenty of water immediately after you plant it will enable the soil to remain moist and settle well around its root balls.

When the top soil starts to dry out, water the young fruit tree with more water. This will enable water to go in deep, and as a result, the fruit tree will have a healthier and deeper root system. Deep watering the fruit tree after every three days in the first two seasons will lead to a healthy and strong fruit tree.

Overwatering or **waterlogging** a young fruit tree in a pot can affect the root growth. Irregular watering can make some fruit trees bolt. which will result in growth of a poor and weak fruit tree.

Watering Mature Trees

Although mature trees require less water compared to baby trees, they regularly need a thorough watering to have juicy fruits. You can use drip irrigation to keep the soil moist and encourage a healthy root development. The tree will also be able to produce more juicy fruits.

Watering During Summer Periods

You need to keep the fruit tree soil moist and not waterlogged and continue watering the fruit tree until the harvest time. During the summer, water the fruit trees when at least 8 to 10 inches of the topsoil goes dry. Some fruit trees, like citrus, need to be watered when at least 3 to 4 inches of the top soil dries out.

During hot weather, you need to water them more often to ensure the fruit tree produces juicier fruits.

The amount of water needed depends on the fruit type, tree size, stage of growth, and temperature within the greenhouse or outdoors if transplanted outside. Fruits grown in sandy soil need watering almost daily during the summer because sandy soil does not retain water for long.

You may consider adding compost to the sandy soil to aid in retaining moisture. Alternatively, if you have planted the fruits on clay soil, you need to water the fruit tree more often. Be careful not to waterlog the tree, as clay soil is more prone to waterlogging.

To know how much water each fruit tree requires per day, you can use a **controlled drip irrigation**.

Drip irrigation helps in stabilizing the fruit tree's growth and maintains the quality of its fruit production. Water requirement is an important component for fruits grown in tropical and subtropical areas, and it determines the mass production of the fruit tree and the fruit quality.

Mulching the Fruit Tree

Farmers using a mulching process to improve the soil underneath. There are different materials you can use to improve the soil condition, and the type of material to use depends on the kind of soil in your garden.

You can apply a mulch to your fruit tree garden or even flower beds to grow a healthier fruit tree and keep away weeds or grass. Mulching makes the fruits drought resistant, as the practice helps the mulched soil retain more water. There will also be less weeding, watering, and even fewer pest problems.

Mulch can be in the form of wood chips or bark pieces, and you should pour natural mulch in circles to cover the whole root system. Mulching 3 to 4 inches deep discourages the growth of weeds around the fruit tree area. Apply mulch with care and do not cover the tree trunk or stems.

Sometimes, mulch can retain moisture. If that moisture piles up against the tree trunk or the stems, it can cause them to rot.

Why You Should Mulch Trees

- Helps in insulating the soil and protects the tree roots from heat and extreme cold.

- Helps retain water in the soil, and as a result, the roots can stay moist for longer.

- Enables you to create a stable, cool, and moist environment surrounding the root system.

- Protects the fruit tree from damage caused by lawnmowers.

- Reduces competition

- from the surrounding plants, such as grass and weeds.

GREENHOUSE

How to Maintain Fruit Tree Health

During the first two years of planting the tree, you should give the fruit tree extra care by watering and fertilizing.

Always water the tree deeply at least twice or thrice per week to encourage deep root development. If you have planted the fruit tree in a rocky area with fast draining soil, you should water the tree root ball and the surrounding soil regularly.

You should also inspect the fruit tree often. Be sure to look at:

- **The leaf size of the fruit**—indicates any change.

- **New leaves or buds**—indicates change compared to previous buds or leaves.

- **Trunk decay or any deformation**—indicates stem decay or a problem that has been affecting the tree from a young age.

- **Curled leaves**—can indicate fungi or pest infection especially if on new leaves.

- Any twig growth.

Fruit Tree Pollination

Pollination is an important factor in fruit production process. Without pollination, your plants would produce few fruit. Pollination is the process of transferring pollen from the male parts to the stigma in the female parts of a plant. Most plants are either self-pollinators, or they rely on insect and wind pollinators.

Pollinators can transfer pollen either within the same flower or across flowers in different plant species.

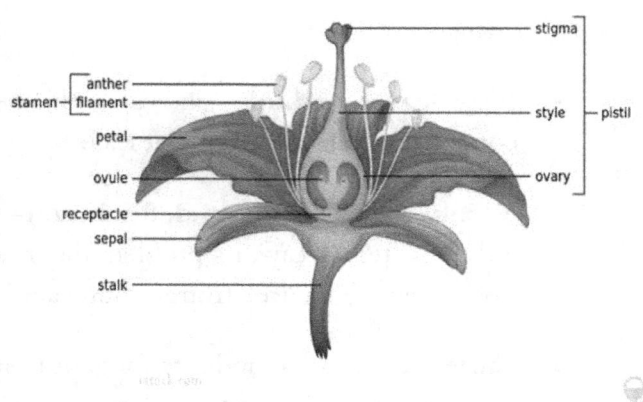

Fruit trees require pollination to produce fruits. The majority of fruit-tree species do not self-pollinate;

therefore, they need pollinators to aid in the pollination process.

Pollination can either be:

- Wind or insect pollination
- Self-pollination by use of a pollen sprayer or hand pollination
- Cross pollination

In **cross pollination**, a plant pollinates another plant of different species to produce a **genetic plant**. Fruit tree cross pollination will produce a fruit with characteristics from two pollinating plants.

Fruits cross pollinated by insects produce more fruits than self-pollinated fruits, and bees are the main fruit tree pollinators.

Some plants that need insect pollinators to make the fruit juice include:

- Watermelons
- Apples
- Blackberries
- Blueberries
- Raspberries

- Pears
- Cucumber
- Plums

Other fruits are **self-pollinating** and do not require any other plants to pollinate their flowers. In this type of pollination, pollination occurs on the same flower.

Chapter Summary

Since fruits do well in cool, humid, and mild winters, growing them in a greenhouse will give them an adequate temperature to enhance their growth. You can also adjust the temperatures of the structure. The greenhouse can protect the fruit trees from wind damage too, especially citrus, which is a fruit that cannot tolerate the wind.

Planting free-standing fruits requires you to dig a large hole and add compost manure or horse manure to the soil and cover the mixture. Monitor the soil temperature and when the temperature drops to 85°F (29°C), then you can add seeds to the seedling trays.

Always monitor the temperature to ensure they don't drop 85°F (29°C).

The ideal soil for growing fruits should be well-drained with loam texture. Fruits also need a deep root system, so a deep soil with topsoil of at least 3 feet is highly recommended. You should also test the soil to know the type present in your garden or yard, so you can know the adjustments to make to the pH level and nutrient value of the soil. Most fruits need a 6 to 6.5 pH balance.

In the next chapter, you will learn how to cultivate vegetables.

CHAPTER FIVE

CULTIVATING VEGETABLES

Greenhouses are an ideal place to cultivate vegetables all year round. It allows you to start off the vegetable garden without waiting for a particular season. You can also harvest some vegetables early, such as French beans.

During the summer months, you can grow vegetables like cucumbers, tomatoes, peppers, and chillies. Some of these vegetables are low maintenance and easy to plant in your backyard.

Greenhouses provide you with a controlled environment where you can try other heat-loving vegetables like sweet potatoes, okra, and melons. You don't have to worry about the climatic conditions of your location—with the various greenhouse tools and accessories, you can plant almost anything anywhere.

You can also take advantage of the autumn sun and plant salad crops and French beans.

GREENHOUSE

Although the optimum temperature for most plants is between 75°F to 85°F (24°C to 29°C), vegetables like cabbage, broccoli, and peas can grow in temperatures below 40°F (4°C). Tomatoes and peppers grow well within 80°F to 85°F (27°C to 29°C) temperature range.

Getting Started

You can start small when planting your vegetables. If you haven't bought the containers and pots to plant seeds, you can improvise by getting clear plastic containers like the ones used for grapes or any other fresh fruits in a supermarket. The clear lid will act as a container for planting the seeds, which you can cover with a plastic wrap.

Based on the size of your greenhouse structure, you can plant multiple seeds on the benches or on the shelves. After planting, you can add and install lighting and other temperature control equipment in the greenhouse. You can use fluorescent lights to increase the amount of light in the greenhouse while boasting seedling growth.

Sometimes, it is good to disinfect the benches, shelves, pots, and trays before planting seeds on them. The moist environment inside can attract pests like fungi, algae, among others.

How to Grow Vegetables in the Greenhouse

Vegetables grown in your own garden will be the freshest. You can extend the growing season of spring and autumn by growing them in your greenhouse at any time. A greenhouse will allow you to control the temperature, humidity, water, and light, based on the needs of the vegetables. The type of vegetables to grow in your greenhouse will depend on your location and the temperatures within your greenhouse garden.

To succeed in cultivating vegetables, you must:

1. *Planning*

GREENHOUSE

Planning involves preparation of the seeding area in the greenhouse. You need to determine how much space you require for the growing beds and the grow bags' floor space. Ensure the greenhouse has enough space to separate spring plants from the summer vegetables you're planning to grow.

Prepare the benches to create more room for seedlings. You can move some crops outside during the summer to create more room for planting other vegetables.

2. Planting the Seeds

Plant the seeds in the pots or starting tray. Read all the instructions on the seed packet and follow the instructions to plant the seeds, then make sure to buy high-quality seeds from a trusted source. Seeds of high quality will increase the germination rate.

Put two to three seeds in a pot containing the seed-starting mix and avoid using regular soil, as it may contain some diseases or may not be good for the germination of the seeds. Water the pots by using a sprayer or a meat-basting syringe, and gently water the pot without causing soil disruption. After watering, cover the pot with a plastic material to prevent it from drying too quickly.

The seed-starting mix provides the best conditions for germination of the seeds. It is best for drainage and has an excellent water-holding capacity. It also minimizes diseases, which can affect any vulnerable seedlings.

The containers should have an adequate number of holes to facilitate draining and ensure the seeds are not waterlogged. You should keep the seed-starting mix moist at all times to allow the seeds receive enough air and water, which are essential for the seeds' growth.

Once you plant the seeds, place the pots or trays where there is direct sunlight. If the greenhouse has little sunlight, you can supplement it with artificial lights, such as a fluorescent light.

After the seedlings emerge, ensure the pots have good access to light and control the greenhouse temperatures according to the needs of the seedlings.

You can use a heated propagator to increase the warmth needed for the crop germination.

3. Growing the Vegetables

After the seedling show up, remove the plastic cover and put them where they can access light, as they will need a lot of light and a frost-free environment to continue growing. You need to ensure some sections of the greenhouse are properly heated to provide enough of a warm environment for the plants' growth, especially for tender vegetables.

GREENHOUSE

Monitor the temperature of the greenhouse at all times. Some vegetables like broccoli grow within 50°F to 70°F (10°C to 21°C) during the day and between 45°F and 55°F (7°C and 13°C) at night. Warm-loving vegetables can tolerate day temperatures between 60°F and 85°F (16°C and 29°C) and 55°F to 65°F (13°C to 18°C) for night temperatures. Therefore, warm and cool vegetables may not survive in the same greenhouse temperatures, so you should always choose what to grow in each greenhouse and when.

You should also start the fertilization of the growing seedlings after every week. Organic fertilizers are highly recommended because they can provide a wide range of nutrients and micronutrients to the seedling.

If there are more seedlings in the pot, you can thin out the excess seedlings with scissors once the seedling has grown two sets of leaves. Always thin out the *weakest* one.

Each pot or container should have a single seedling for it to grow well, so continue to water the seedlings to allow them to grow.

4. Transplanting the Vegetable Seedlings

You need to plant the vegetable seedlings in their final location once they're well rooted in the soil. You can do this using large containers or growing bags to plant the crops. Offer extra care to the newly transplanted vegetables and ensure they're shaded from direct sunlight for a day or two or until they get established.

When transplanting the vegetable plants, make sure you place the pots with the tallest plants on the shelves at the back.

Ensure there is some space between each vegetable plant and water the vegetables regularly or when necessary. You should not leave the top soil dry for too long.

You must give vegetables like cucumbers and melons support as they climb up. You can tie one cucumber tree to another to give them more strength and to allow them to support one another. To support cordon tomatoes, tie them up with strings or canes.

5. Maintenance

Make sure you water the vegetables well and daily, as uneven watering can affect some of the vegetables. For example, if certain sections of the tomato beds are not well-watered, it can result in rotting.

Ensure the greenhouse is well-ventilated and there is enough light inside to aid in the growth of the vegetables. You can install automatic vents or use the manual vents to keep the room well-ventilated.

GREENHOUSE

You can open the door of the greenhouse or its windows to let fresh and cool air flow inside, which will help regulate the greenhouse's temperature. If there is too much heat lost in the greenhouse, you can reduce the heat loss by insulating all windows and doors.

If you have planted warm-loving vegetables such as cucumber or okra, make sure the vents remain closed and increase the humidity in the room. This makes certain that no moisture is retained, which can damage the vegetables. You can also partition some parts of the greenhouse with a clear, plastic material.

Make sure you keep the greenhouse clean at all times. Investing in bubble wrap insulation for your structure would be an excellent idea to address this concern.

If you're using a heated greenhouse, install a thermostat to maintain the greenhouse's temperature. This will ensure the minimum nighttime temperatures do not drop below the expected temperatures for the plants' growth. You should also install a two thermometers to monitor the minimum and maximum temperatures within the greenhouse. One thermometer will measure the temperature inside the greenhouse, whereas the second thermometer will measure the outdoor temperatures.

Always remember to tie up the vegetables to provide support for any new growth, especially if you are handling tomatoes in the greenhouse.

Be alert and watch out for pests, bugs, fungi, and any other diseases that can affect the plants in the greenhouse. If a fungal disease infects your garden, you should consult with professional services on the possible insect repellents to use.

Challenges You May Face

You may face soil problems like soil borne diseases, especially if you have been cultivating on the same type of soil for more than four years. Therefore, if you're growing vegetables in the greenhouse border, you can reduce the soil borne diseases by digging out the soil and replacing it with new soil or using a good garden loam.

You can try **grafted plants** if you have soil issues in your garden. In this case, tomatoes and aubergines will do well.

Another way you can reduce the soil borne diseases is by using pots and grow bags. You should cover the soil with a plastic sheeting, then place the pot or grow bag on top of it.

GREENHOUSE

Some diseases that can affect the growth of your vegetables include: grey mould, powdery mildew, and damping off.

Some pests that may affect the vegetables include: glasshouse leafhoppers, red spider mites, and glasshouse whiteflies.

What Vegetables to Plant and When

For your greenhouse to stay productive all year round, you need to take advantage of every plant growing season and diversify your garden.

Winter and Early Spring

GREENHOUSE

If you have installed a heated greenhouse, you can plant **tomatoes** and **peppers** in one section of your garden. Use a heated propagator to aid in the germination of the vegetables.

You can plant frost tolerant vegetables like **cabbage**, **lettuce**, **onions**, **Brussels sprouts**, and **peas** as you wait for the warm weather. These vegetables can survive in low temperatures, and you can transplant them outdoors.

Mid-Spring Season

In mid-spring, you can prepare your garden to plant tender vegetables like **cucumbers**, **melons**, **pumpkins**, **courgettes**, and **sweetcorn**. Later, you would transplant the vegetables during the late spring or plant them outside in the early summer period.

These vegetables require a warm and more controlled environment for them to grow well, so install a heated propagator to ensure proper germination of the vegetables. If the plants are exposed to any front before you transplant them outdoors in the early summer, they will not survive the frost.

Early Summer Season

GREENHOUSE

The summer season includes late spring and early summer season. During this season, you can transplant the mid-spring vegetables outdoors and create more space for planting midsummer vegetables.

When temperatures are favorable, you can plant **eggplants**, **hot peppers** and **tomatoes** in the garden. Although these are heat-loving plants, too much heat can affect some vegetables' growth and invite some molds in the greenhouse. It can also make some vegetables dry out.

You can transfer the vegetables outside once the frost is over.

In midsummer, you can harvest some of the vegetables grown like **cucumbers**, **melons**, and **French beans**.

Late Summer

During this season, you can plant more **potatoes** in the greenhouse. You can also grow **lettuce**, **carrots**, and **spicy salad leaves** to take advantage of the autumn sun and harvest some of the vegetables.

Autumn Season

Some activities done during this period include harvesting some of the vegetables grown in summer. You can grow **lettuce** in a grow bags and harvest them during the winter season. Other vegetables you can grow during this period include the **French beans**, **snow peas**, **kale**, and **calabrese**.

How to Determine the Best Soil for Planting Vegetables

Cultivating a strong soil foundation will enable you to harvest healthy and nutritious vegetables. Healthy soil with result in healthy vegetable and a healthy environment.

If you plant vegetables on a healthy soil, your cost for fertilization and pesticides will be less, and it will not only result in healthier vegetables, but it will also improve your own health.

A good organic soil is full of humus and is made from decomposed materials such as leaves, compost, and grass clippings. The decomposed materials increase nutrient and mineral values of the organic soil, making it ideal for growing plants.

Soil requirements for most vegetables are the same; although, there are certain types of vegetables that do better in certain types of soils. In this tutorial, I will discuss the general soil requirement for greenhouse garden. The best soil for cultivating vegetables is one that drains well and loose.

Determining Soil Health

Plants need nutrients like nitrogen, potassium, and phosphorus for their growth. We commonly term these nutrients as the **primary micronutrients** that plants absorb from the soil. Other nutrients like magnesium, calcium, and sulfur are referred to as the **secondary nutrients**. Although there are other nutrients present in a healthy soil, these are the most common nutrients and each performs a certain function in the growth of a plant.

Soil health can also be determined inform of its pH value; that is, you can have an acidic soil or an alkaline soil based on the pH reading. All the nutrients, soil texture, and soil pH contribute to making healthy soil.

Soil Testing

Soil testing is done to determine which minerals are present or lacking and the percentage of each mineral concentration. The tests measures soil pH, basic nutrients like calcium, potassium, magnesium, pHospHorus, nitrogen, and micronutrient content.

Most vegetables need a pH value of between 6 to 7. If the pH value is greater than 7, you need to lower the pH; if it's below 6, you have to raise the pH. The soil pH affects the growth of vegetables, and no matter how many nutrients the soil may have, the plants will not absorb the nutrients if the pH is outside of the recommended range.

You can test the soil pH to determine whether its alkaline or acidic using pH test kits available in the market.

To get the accurate result on soil components and nutrients, it's best you test them during spring or fall season. This will enable you to know the soil components and whether to add any fertilizers to the soil or not.

You can balance the pH by:

Reducing soil acidity: If the test shows the soil has high acidity, you need to reduce excess acidity in the soil. One way of reducing acidity level is mixing the soil with limestone. Make sure to follow the manufacturer's instructions on the quantity you're supposed to use for every mix. You can add limestone each year at the beginning of every fall or during spring.

Increasing the pH level: When the soil is alkaline, you can add some additives like sulfur or gypsum to increase its pH. You can also apply compost material to the soil regularly to reduce its alkalinity. Make sure to always test the soil every time you add compost; otherwise, you may make the soil too acidic.

Soil Texture and Type

Apart from examining the soil pH, nutrients, and micronutrients, you need to determine its texture and type.

You would determine the by the amount of sand, silt, and clay present in the soil. Most soils have **sand** as its highest constituent, so when touched, it feels gritty. That is followed by **silt**, which is slippery when wet and looks powdery when dry. The component with the lowest constituent in is **clay**, with pieces that tend to stack together and look like sheets of paper.

You can buy a complete soil testing kit from any hardware store like Home Depot, or retail shops like Walmart. Make sure to follow the manufacturer's instructions to test the soil. Alternatively, you can determine whether the soil is sandy or silt with your hands. Pick some soil up from your garden and rub it together with your fingers—if the soil feels gritty, then it is probably sandy soil; if it feels smooth like powder, then it is silt. However, if it feels slippery or sticky when wet, or harsh when dry, then it is clay soil.

Sandy soil is poor in nutrients and drains quicker due to its large particles. The soil also has a low number of micronutrients and organic matter, which are essential components for plants to thrive. Therefore, if you have this type of soil in your garden, consider improving its texture and nutrients before planting the vegetables.

Silty soil is more fertile and has all the nutrients and micronutrients required by the plants to grow, but it drains poorly.

Clay soil is dense, and plants may not grow well in this type of soil. There is no space between the clay particles affecting its drainage, and you will need to improve the soil to make it appropriate for plant growth.

Improving Soil

You can improve garden soil by adding organic matter. You can do this by adding compost and manure, or through mulching and growing cover crops. Adding organic matter to the soil will supply all the nutrients the plants need to grow, and it is the most recommended.

You can also add mulch and some green manure to make the soil healthier for vegetable growth. Adding fertilizers to the soil will only increase some nutrients in the soil and will not be ideal for maintaining it.

A good soil should have enough air held between its particles. Plants need air for their overall growth and photosynthesis. The amount of air in the soils has atmospheric nitrogen, which converts into a form used by the plants as they grow. Oxygen in the soil is also essential for the survival of certain soil organisms that contribute to the plants' growth.

Silt and clay soils has little air between the small particles, which are close together. You can increase the amount of air circulation between the particles by digging the soil to make it loose and mixing it with compost.

Sandy soil has big particles that allow a lot of air in. The only problem with sandy soil, however, is the rapid decomposition of the compost organic matter caused by excess air in the soil particles.

Adding organic matter to the soil helps balance the air supply in the soil, and most plants can grow well in soils with 25% of air. Organic matter can break the heavy particles of clay and silt soils and bind together the particles in sandy soil. This process helps improve the air supply in the soil and improve its retention of water and nutrients. Organic compost can also lower the pH level of the soil and create an environment perfect for growing vegetables.

Adding Fertilizers to the Soil

Organic fertilizers are the best compared to the synthetic fertilizers, but they take a long time before you can realize the benefits. They provide long-term supply of nutrients to the plants. Alternatively, you can use synthetic fertilizers, which only add nutrients to the soil for a short period of time. However, frequent use of synthetic fertilizers can have a negative impact on the soil in the long run, since liquid or dry fertilizers can kill all the microorganisms in the soil.

When adding fertilizers, follow the instructions on the label. You would mix dry fertilizer with the soil, according to the direction given, and once done with mixing them, you can water the soil. Different fertilizers have different a nutrient constituent, and each has the nutrients listed on the label.

If you're using liquid fertilizers, spray it directly to the plant or on the soil. Fish emulsion and seaweed blends are the most common liquid fertilizers in the market. Always read the instructions of every fertilizer before using it.

Watering Vegetables

Plants need water to survive, and vegetables are no exception. You should ensure you water the vegetable plants moderately to gain maximum yield.

Vegetables are best watered in the morning, which ensures full absorption of water by the vegetable roots. If you water during midday sun, there is a high chance of water evaporation before absorption. Watering at night encourages the growth of slugs and can introduce diseases such as blackspot and others.

You will need thorough watering to grow strong and healthy vegetables. Doing so ensures water penetrates deep into the soil, encouraging deep root development. A shallow watering at the surface will result in a weak and shallow root system.

Overwatering can create a perfect environment for growing diseases and encourage snails in the area, and excess water that runs off the soil can wash away soil nutrients, making the plants growing in that location have a weak and shallow root system.

If the soil doesn't drain well and you leave the vegetables in a waterlogged area for long, it will deprive them of oxygen, which is an essential component for their growth.

GREENHOUSE

Always check the soil moisture to avoid overwatering the vegetables. If you grow the vegetables in containers or pots, ensure the containers have enough water drainage holes.

Seedlings require extra care. You need to keep the soil for planting the vegetables moist, and once you plant the seeds in the soil, carefully water them to avoid washing the seeds away. As the seeds grow, you can introduce drip irrigation to have a controlled watering. Another method is to dip the pot with the growing plant into a tray with water, which will allow the pot to soak water from below rather than watering from above. When the pot is fully soaked, you can remove it from the water tray and leave it to drain.

GREENHOUSE

Sometimes, too much or too little water may make crops wither. If the soil above and below the surface is dry, you should water the crops immediately. If the crops are in an area where they experience direct sun, you can move the containers toward some shade or shade the entire area.

If the crops are withering due to excess water, check the drainage system. If the crops are on waterlogged soil, you can create more holes in the soil to aid in draining more water.

When planting, you should also group thirsty vegetables together to make your watering more efficient. Some thirsty vegetables include:

- Carrots
- Cucumbers
- Peas
- Beans
- Peppers
- Pumpkins

Pollination in Vegetables

Vegetables are self-pollinating plants and do not require insects or any animal pollinators to make their crops.

GREENHOUSE

A self-pollinating plant has both the **stamen** (from the male parts) and the **pistil** in the flower. A gentle breeze can transfer the male stamen to the female pistil, and once the pollinators come across these flowers, they facilitate the pollination process. In this type of pollination, you will find both the male and female flower parts on the same flower.

If there are no pollinators, you can complete the pollination process through hand pollination by either tapping on the vegetable stems or brushing your hands against the flowers as you walk by.

Some self-pollinating vegetables include:

- Eggplants
- Peppers

- Tomatoes
- Legumes, like beans and peas

Other plants that use cross pollination require the wind to move the male pollen (stamen) to the female pistil. They pollinate the flowers in the plant or use flowers from another plant.

Some wind pollinated plants include:

- Corn
- Wheat
- Oats
- Spinach
- Chard

Plants that grow from their roots and leaves require no pollination at all. This is because they do not depend on any flowers or seeds.

Some of these plants include:

- Potatoes
- Onions
- Carrots
- Broccoli

- Cauliflower

- Garlic

- Lettuce

All these vegetables grow only for their roots or the plant as a whole, like lettuce, and you should not pollinate them. If any of these vegetables grow flowers, you must remove them immediately.

Vegetables in the family of **cucurbit**, for example—cucumbers, pumpkins, muskmelon, and squash—require bee pollination because they have separate male and female flowers. Most of these vegetables have either the male flowers or the female flowers; therefore, they require pollinators to transfer the male pollen to the female stigma. If there are no pollinators, you can use a hand pollination.

With hand pollination, use a clean paintbrush to harvest pollen from the male flower, then transfer it to the stigma of the female flower. Always make sure to do hand pollination in the *morning*.

Animal pollinators can provide you with a long-term solution for pollinating cucurbit-type vegetables. Attract animal pollinators to your garden by creating a pollinator habitat within the yard or nearby to attract bees.

Examples of insect-pollinated vegetables include:

- Cabbage
- Kale
- Cucumbers
- Muskmelons
- Okra
- Celery

When using self-pollination on your vegetables, you produce **true-to-type vegetables**. That is, vegetables with the same size, color, flavor, and shape as the parent plant.

Cross-pollinated vegetables may produce a true-to-type vegetable, and sometimes, the crop may not grow to true after pollination.

Causes of Poor Pollination

Sometimes, the vegetables can have too many flowers but yield few fruits. This can be due to poor pollination, possibly caused by:

- **Poor weather**: In cold areas, there are fewer insects to pollinate your plants; therefore, you must rely on hand pollination.

GREENHOUSE

- **Frost**: If you're in an area that experiences frost, and you do not have enough heating equipment to regulate the temperatures, then the frost will affect the flowers and ruin the pollination process. You can solve this problem by spraying the flowers in the morning with ice cold water, which will slow down the rate of warming up the flowers and make them sprout out gently.

- **Access of insects**: Pollination may not take place because insects cannot access the greenhouse. You can keep the greenhouse open during sunny days to allow insects inside to pollinate the plants.

Chapter Summary

In this chapter, we went over various strategies for cultivating vegetables in the greenhouse. The chapter highlighted specific ways to:

- To plant vegetables using seeds in the greenhouse garden.

- Determine the best soil for planting vegetables, how to test the soil nutrients, how to determine the soil type and texture, and how to improve the soil.

- What to plant in the greenhouse and when.

- How to water vegetables.

- How pollination takes place in the greenhouse.

In the next chapter, you will learn how to cultivate herbs in the greenhouse.

CHAPTER SIX

CULTIVATING HERBS

Have you ever wanted to grow your own herbs in your backyard? With a greenhouse, growing herbs is completely possible, and there are various designs and styles you can choose from.

Growing your own herbs ensures you have a constant supply of fresh herbs in your garden, which will serve you with medicinal and culinary benefits. They can help cure colds and boost your sleep, among curing diseases.

Herbs can also add taste and flavor to a variety of foods. You can use different herbs to produce different spices for adding taste to food.

You would not only add these herbs to your food, but you can also produce attractive flowers that make your garden look more beautiful.

Growing herbs is easy, as you only need to set up a greenhouse structure and you are good to go. Once you build a greenhouse to cultivate herbs, always remember cultivating herbs in the greenhouse is different from growing herbs outdoors because greenhouse plants require more attention than the outdoor plants.

Growing herbs in a greenhouse will allow you to:

Extend the herbs growing period: A greenhouse provides you with a controlled temperature environment that will allow you to plant herbs at any time, meaning that you will be able to grow and sell a lot of out-of-season herbs. Whether growing the herbs for personal use or sale, a greenhouse garden will ensure you have a constant supply.

Protect the herbs from pests: Having your own controlled greenhouse environment to plant herbs means don't have to worry about pests and other diseases affecting crops in the neighborhood. You can take measures to ensure you herbs stay safe from insects, rodents, and caterpillars.

Protect the herbs from harsh weather conditions: Greenhouses protect crops from extreme heat, strong winds, dust storms, and other harsh weather conditions. You can grow any crop in any unpredictable climate, provided you have all the equipment and tools needed to operate the greenhouse.

Prevent soil erosion: Another benefit of using a greenhouse is to protect your crops from any damage caused by flash floods, rainstorms, or any other condition that may affect the crops if left exposed.

Tips for Growing Herbs

Herbs can grow in any location, even in areas where there is freezing temperatures. All you need is a sheltered place or a greenhouse where you can control these extreme temperatures and extend the herbs' growing season.

To get healthy, all-year-round herbs you need to:

1. **Water them regularly:** Always water herbs until the soil is moist, then leave them to dry out slightly before the next

watering. From watering, they will develop a deep root system.

2. **Let them remain dormant for a while:** During the cold season, herbs are dormant; therefore, don't worry if you see the herbs perennial varieties turn brown at the top during that period. After a while, you can trim the brown parts and leave them to grow to their usual size during the spring season.

3. **Maintain fresh air in the greenhouse:** Ensure there is circulation of fresh air inside the greenhouse. You can open the door and greenhouse windows to let fresh air in or install vents. If you locate your greenhouse in a moist and wet environment, the stale air inside may encourage fungus and pests in the greenhouse. To avoid this potential outcome, keep the greenhouse well-ventilated and ensure there is a lot of fresh air inside.

4. **Pinch the herbs:** Pinching the flowing stem will keep the herb well-trimmed and bushy. It also prevents it from growing to seed and extends the herbs growing period. When flowers and seeds show up,

it will automatically slow down the plants growth, and you will only be able to see a few leaves.

Basic Requirements for Herb Growth

Regardless of which herbs you want to grow in your greenhouse, there are various requirements for all herbs.

Setting up a greenhouse will enable you to grow all-year round herbs and control moisture, head, and shade for the herbs. However, the largest problem with herbs is lack of adequate moisture in the garden area. Therefore, you need to ensure there is adequate supply of moisture for the herb plants to succeed. To increase moisture, you must install a misting system and automatic drip hoses in the greenhouse. An automatic hose system makes sure that there is a frequent supply of water to facilitate the steady growth of herbs.

A system of shading the herb plants is another key component for the success of your herbs. If you already have an existing greenhouse, you can create a shading system by attaching rip-stop nylon or Velcro to the roof of the greenhouse. You can easily attach them with hooks and remove them when necessary.

GREENHOUSE

When building a new greenhouse for growing herbs, don't roof it entirely with glass or plexiglass. You can roof some sections of the greenhouse with sunroof-type installations or use skylights, which are great for providing adequate air circulation in the greenhouse.

Set up artificial lights raised 2 to 4 inches away from the herbs. Herbs grow well in grow lights, which make the herb plants adapt easier to an outdoor climate.

Use the seed-starting mix to grow the herbs' seeds. The starting mix is lighter than the normal potting soil and makes the seeds germinate quicker. The starting mix increases the seeds' chances of survival and reduces the chance for infectious diseases, which can be caused by potting soil.

Plastic trays are the best for growing herb seeds, and the trays have small cells that make it easy to grow many herbs at a time. If you have herbs with the same growth requirements, you can grow them in the same area but in different sections.

You can transplant the herbs later into large clay pots. If you're planting herbs that do not require any transplant like Parsley, you can use a large clay pot when planting the seeds. Keep pots and seed trays in a warm area and away from direct sunlight.

Once you plant the seeds, cover them with a plastic wrap to keep the soil moist and speed up the germination process. After germination, remove the plastic cover and keep the trays in an area in which can access light.

If you want to keep the seedlings green and the roots strong, you can spray the herb plant with a light liquid organic fertilizer. You should do this one week after the germination of the seeds.

Growing herbs from their seeds is the most common procedure. There is a wide range of seeds to choose from, with some suppliers selling organic seeds and others selling non-GMO seeds. Some herbs are also bee friendly.

Another option is to plant the herbs from their cuttings. You can cut a piece of an already-grown plant and plant it in a different place or share it with your neighbors.

How to Grow Herbs From Seeds

Growing herbs requires little maintenance once it is well-established. Each harvest produces an enough number of herbs you can use for a long time. Fresh herbs directly from the garden have a fresh fragrance and can add more flavor to your food.

GREENHOUSE

You should grow herbs in a specific section in the greenhouse. Giving you more room to grow other vegetables.

You can cultivate herbs from seeds in your greenhouse, and growing herbs from their seeds is less expensive compared to buying herb seedlings. You will also have a wide variety of herbs to plant.

Planting the Seeds

1. You should soak the herbs' seeds in water for a whole day or leave them to soak in a container with water overnight.

GREENHOUSE

2. Prepare the containers for planting the seeds and make sure the containers or pots have enough holes to drain water. Then, fill the container with the start mix soil.

3. Plant the seeds in the container with the start mix soil. You need to plant these seeds three times deeper than the normal seed planting depth. If the seeds are tiny, you can press them into the soil with your hands.

   Water the seeds, then cover the container with a plastic wrap. This will help retain moisture in the soil mix and speed up the seeds' growth.

   You should take a lot of care when watering the planted seeds to avoid washing them away, and you can use a bottle springle sprayer to thoroughly water them while avoiding this outcome. Once you've watered them, you need not water them again until the seedlings appear.

   Place the planted seeds in the container in an area with access to light.

4. Once the seeds grow, remove the plastic cover and water the seedlings. Ensure the

containers are in a warm area and have access to sunlight.

5. If you have excess seedlings in a container, you can wait until two sets of leaves emerge, then remove the weak seedlings. If you want to transfer the seedlings to your garden, you can take the containers outside when the temperatures are warm to harden them. After a week, you can transfer the seedlings to your garden or outdoors.

6. You can also transplant the leaves by digging a hole where you want to transplant them and then pinching off the lower set of leaves on the plant.

The hole you make should be able to hold the plant up to where you had pinched the leaves.

You can then remove the plant from the container and transplant it in the hole. Turn the container upside down and carefully allow the plant to slide into your hands, while avoiding pulling the plant by its stem or leaves. Once you've removed it from the container, you can put it into the hole and add soil around the plant. The leaf nodes made from pinching the lower sets of the leaves will grow roots when transplanted.

Water the plant once daily for a whole week, and thereafter, water them twice on a weekly basis.

When the herb plant gets bushy, add mulch around it to avoid weed growth.

Soil Preparation

Although herbs can do well in almost any type of soil, having a good soil will help you maintain your garden easier. While many herbs will require little care, you will still need to prepare the soil for cultivating herbs in your garden.

A good soil for planting herbs should have 50% of solid material and 50% of porous space to provide enough room for holding air, water, and the herb plant's roots. The solid material comprises inorganic matter made of fine rock particles and organic matter made of decayed plants.

Inorganic soil particles are divided into three parts: Clay, silt, and sand.

Clay has the smallest soil particles among the three, followed by silt with medium-size rock particles, and sand with the largest number of soil particles. The amount of sand, silt, or clay in the soil determines the soil texture. For example, loam soil is a mixture of clay, silt, and sand in the ratio of 20:40:40%.

Soil Texture

To harvest better and healthier herbs, you need to improve the soil texture and structure. You can add organic matter to the soil to help the soil hold or drain more water.

You can use materials like sawdust, grass clippings, corncobs, straw, and cover crops as organic matter, and you can use your own compost as organic matter to enrich the soil nutrients.

Soil Testing

Similar to with vegetables and fruit, you also need to test the soil nutrients and pH level. You can collect soil samples from your garden and send them to a laboratory for testing, or use home soil testing kits that are available in the market. You can buy one and use it to test soil nutrients and pH level.

Home test kits come with an instruction manual for how to use them and how to read the results presented to determine your soil texture and nutrients. Some kits have information on how to get the soil samples for testing. Follow the instructions to test the soil in your garden.

Based on the test report, you can figure out the type of fertilizer to use for increasing soil nutrients in your garden. Test reports from a lab come with recommendations for the amount and type of fertilizer needed to improve the soil.

Soil test results will show the pH level of the soil, which is its acidic and alkaline balance. The pH level is measured on a scale of 1 to 14, with 1 representing more acidic and 14 as the most alkaline, whereas a scale of 7 shows neutral soil. Herbs grow best in a pH level of between 5.5 and 7.5. It will also show the percentage of nitrogen, potassium, and phosphorous in the soil.

The pH level determines the number of nutrients present in the soil. Soil labs test the type of soil, pH level, and the herbs you intend to plant and gives you a recommendation for the pH changes you need to make and the nutrients you should add to the soil to increase herb produce.

According to the pH report, you can adjust the pH level by either raising or lowering it. You can raise the pH by adding lime to the soil at any time of the year, and you can lower the pH level by adding the recommended sulfur product to the soil.

GREENHOUSE

Types of Herbs You Can Grow in a Greenhouse

Tender annual herbs do well in an enclosed greenhouse structure. If you want to extend the growing season for other types of herbs, you can grow them in the greenhouse. Some of these herbs to grow include:

- Basil
- Dill
- Mints
- Lavender
- Parsley
- Chives

- Rosemary
- Thyme
- Cilantro
- Chamomile

Mints are an *invasive herb*; therefore, you must grow it in a container. There are various types of mints you can experiment with in your garden.

When planting herbs like rosemary, lavender, and bay, grow them in raised beds. Their roots may rot when left in moist areas, so ensure that you have good drainage system.

Fertilizing

Herbs grown outdoors require little fertilizer such as adding organic nutrients to boost the nutrients, whereas herbs grown in containers require fertilizers to produce a healthier plant and resist diseases and pests.

Herbs grown in containers use all the nutrients in the soil as they grow, and some nutrients may wash away as you water them. They also dry out quickly compared to those grown in a backyard. However, you can boost the nutrients by adding organic fertilizers to the soil at planting time. As the herb plant grows, you can use liquid fertilizer like fish emulsion to add more nutrients to the plant.

Organic fertilizers from plants and animals may take a lot of time before there is decomposition by microorganisms in the soil to provide nutrients to the plants, whereas inorganic fertilizers provide immediate nutrients to the plants.

Avoid over-fertilizing herbs. Too much fertilizer will result in herbs with bigger plants. It will also affect the essential oils important to adding flavor and aroma of the herb plant, thus diluting its flavor.

Watering Indoor Herbs

Water these herbs regularly. Monitor the herb garden daily, and if you notice the top of the soil dry, you should water the herbs immediately; do *not* overwater them. Overwatering can result to damping, which may make the bottom leaves of the herb to turn yellow.

You can employ an automatic watering system that gives the herbs a certain amount of water each day. This guarantees herbs' growth and makes them healthier.

Always water the roots of the herb and avoid pouring water to the leaves and its stalks because it can encourage fungal infection.

Herbs grown in containers need frequent watering, as the containers dry more quickly. Most herbs require watering three times per week or when an inch of the top soil feels dry. Pots placed outdoors may need daily watering due to the hot sun and wind, which makes the soil dry faster.

When using pots indoors, you can place them on drip trays to hold the water as it drains. Pour away the water from the trays after every irrigation process.

Pollination of Herbs

Some herbs, especially those used to add flavor to the food, do not need pollination. Only the leafy parts or the green part of the plant is needed to add to the food, not its seeds or fruits. However, seed-propagating herbs require pollination to take place to produce viable seeds.

GREENHOUSE

Herbs like thyme, rosemary, parsley, sage, and basil require pollination to produce seeds. Pollination can occur either through insect pollination or hand pollination.

How to Pollinate the Herbs

Stop pruning or pinching the herb leaves and let the herb plant develop flowers.

Once the flowers develop, they will attract insect pollinators like bees into your garden. 75% of herbs grown in a garden attract bee pollinators naturally; therefore, planting some of these herbs in the surrounding environment will attract bee pollinators to your garden. Just leave the greenhouse windows open and pollination will occur naturally.

Alternatively, you can take the herb plant outdoors and place it near other flowers where bees visit more frequently.

Strategies to Boost Pollination

If there is not enough adequate pollination, there will be little produce from the herbs. You can boost more pollination in your garden by attracting more pollinators, using wind pollination, or hand pollination.

1. Plant Flowers to Attract Bees

Bees are attracted to flowers, so planting different types of flowers in the surrounding area will attract different species of bees and other insect pollinators.

Avoid cultivating double flowered plants because they make it difficult for the bees to access the flowers. These plants acts as the natural habitat for the bees, and once drawn into your garden, they will pollinate the herb plants.

Some of the herbs that attract bee pollinators include: basil, sage, lavender, germander, thyme, rosemary, lemon balm, and chamomile.

In an area with good sun and less wind, butterflies can pollinate the herbs. Some herbs that attract butterflies in the garden include: chives, mint, parsley, catmint, and thyme.

2. Wind Pollination

Some herbs rely on wind to carry the male pollen to the female flower. The pollen falls on the female parts, then the pollination takes place. You can facilitate wind movement in the greenhouse by shaking or tapping the plant from its stem.

3. Hands Pollination

Although hand pollination is rarely needed with herbs, you can still use it. During the cold or wet seasons when bees are unavailable, you can use a paintbrush to gather the male pollen and transfer it to the female stigma of the herb flower. You should do this practice early in the morning before the pollen dries up or extreme heat can affect it.

You can also remove the flower and strip off the flower petals, then rub it against a female flower. Make sure you're rubbing on the female flower, as some plants have separate male and female flowers. The female flower has a swelling behind it.

Herbs grown out from cutting, like rosemary and perennial, propagate easier.

Watering Herbs

Just like your vegetables and fruits, herbs require moderate watering. Some herbs only need a single, deep watering per week, while others need regular watering.

Overwatering the herbs will kill them because they cannot handle excess water, and it is one of the principal mistakes many herb gardeners make.

How to Know the Herbs Have Been Overwatered

Herbs thrive well in semi-dry soil, which makes them able to withstand extreme drought in Mediterranean areas or dry climates.

Pay close attention to the herbs—if the herb plants start to wilt but the soil looks wet, you are probably overwatering the herbs. Other signs that can show you're overwatering include:

- The herb leaves turning yellow and starting to fall.

- The leaves turning black or dark in color.

- The herb plant has a fuzzy, mildew substance, like it has been infected with a mildew pathogen.

- The herb roots and stems starting soften and break. Rotted roots due to excess water become a gray or brown color.

- No growth shown, and there is no change to the herb after many days.

- Edema signs appearing, like blisters or lesions, on the herbs' leaves.

If the plant shows any of these signs, check on the drainage system first. If there is any standing water, you need to drain it immediately to avoid rooting of the herb roots and prevent breeding of pests, bacteria, and fungi in the area.

How to Avoid Overwatering

Different herbs require different water needs; therefore, it is essential to group the herbs based on these water needs. There are herbs that require a high amount of water, whereas others need less water. Know which type of herb you want to plant and identify its water needs, as knowing this will enable you to water more herbs more efficiently.

The rule is to water deep once in a while but less frequently. This ensures you grow deep rooted herbs that can withstand any weather condition.

Ensure there is proper drainage even in the potted herbs. If the soil drains poorly, improve the soil drainage by adding organic matter. You should do this before planting the herbs.

Always dip a finger an inch or two into the potting medium; if it's dry, water the herb plant at the root base. This reduces evaporation of water and prevents diseases caused by moisture in the pot media.

Herbs like basil and parsley can help you determine the watering schedule, as they can tell you when they need water by dropping the leaves. Once watered, they spring back to life in minutes. If you neglect them for too long, the leaves turn yellow and there is nothing you can do to recover the herb.

Chapter Summary

Cultivating herbs indoors is simple and enables you to have access to the herbs' medicinal value at your fingertips. Herbs can also add flavor and taste to your food. Whatever location you are in, you can grow any type of herb in your garden or indoors. You can grow herbs from either seeds or seedlings.

Different herbs do well in different types of soil, and determining the best soil for the herbs is essential for increasing their produce. It also helps you figure out the type of herbs to grow and when.

There are insect-attracting herbs you can grow in your garden for which you won't have to worry about pollination.

A wide range of herbs can survive in almost any type of soil and require less fertilization. When grown indoors, the herbs are less infected by insects and pests. You should also water the herbs regularly.

Herbs require extra care when watering. Always make sure you're not overwatering them and that you have good drainage system in place.

In the next chapter, you will learn how to maintain the greenhouse.

CHAPTER SEVEN

MAINTAINING YOUR GREENHOUSE

Installing the greenhouse and planting crops on it is not all you must do—you must also keep the greenhouse in tip-top shape! You would do this with regular cleaning and maintenance of the greenhouse.

Once every year, carry out a thorough cleaning of the greenhouse, as a high amount of moisture and dampness can lead to the growth of fungus, molds, algae, or mildew on the greenhouse walls. If left unchecked for a long time, they can spread throughout the entire greenhouse and infect the crops.

These molds and fungi not only infect the crops, but they can also cause health problems to individuals. Therefore, periodic maintenance of the greenhouses is crucial for the growth of healthy crops and maintaining one's own health too.

How to Maintain the Greenhouse

Remove Bugs and Pests

Wash all the benches in the garden with soapy water. Washing the benches and any other table in the greenhouse will enable you to remove dirt and moisture that can cause mold.

Always ensure you keep the surface of the greenhouse dry, and you can use cloth or a sponge to wipe clean any moisture or damp areas on the surface. Spray any built up mildew on the walls with the mildew spray. You should also clean the area between the panes to avoid buildup of condensation, which can lead to a growth of molds and algae.

GREENHOUSE

Clean the flooring area of your structure thoroughly. Some floors are made of wood, gravel, cement, or fabric carpeting, and depending on your greenhouse's floor type, molds can grow. You need to scrub the floor and clean out any mold, mud, and other decaying matter.

Remove any dead plant branches and leaves. Pests or bugs can infect plants, causing the leaves to wither, and prune any dead leaves or branches to prevent further spread of the disease. You must take the dead leaves out of the greenhouse as soon as possible because if left inside, they may decompose and allow pests or bugs into the greenhouse.

Weeds and any other unimportant plants around the greenhouse area should be removed.

If some pests invade your greenhouse, you can release spiders and ladybugs into the garden, if they are available in your area. If ladybugs are not available in your pet stores, you can use pesticide to deal with pests in the greenhouse instead.

GREENHOUSE

Provide Shade and More Sun

Most greenhouse roofs and windows are made of plastic material or fiberglass. After some time, these materials can turn a darker shade caused by overheating from sun or microscopic molds. This change can reduce the amount of light into the greenhouse.

You should periodically clean the windows to allow more light and sun enter the greenhouse. Consider replacing the roof material after a while.

Plant trees that can provide shade for your greenhouse during the summer months, which can act as shade to protect your plants from hot weather. You should plant the trees on the west side of the greenhouse to block the sun and excess light into the structure. During the winter, the trees shed off the leaves, which allows extra sun to get into the greenhouse.

Alternatively, you can install roll-up shades. Roll-up shades are closed during the summer to protect the plants from the sun and remain opened in winter to allow more sun and light enter.

GREENHOUSE

Heating and Ventilation Problems

Greenhouses provide a temperature-controlled environment to meet the needs of your plants. You need to maintain the heating and ventilation equipment and ensure they're working properly. Check the equipment regularly and do full maintenance on them before the winter growing season.

If there are any gaps in the greenhouse exterior, you can use new glass panes to fill out the large holes or caulk to fill small holes in the exterior. This ensures heat you maintain heat inside the greenhouse.

Paint all walls black, as doing so makes sure that you attract and retain more heat.

GREENHOUSE

You can install roof vents between the ceiling and the rooftop. In most greenhouses, hot air is always trapped at the top part of the ceiling and prevent the crops from receiving enough warmth. Installing vents can easily push away hot air and allow fresh air from the outside in, thus increasing fresh air circulation inside.

You can also use fans installed diagonally at the opposite corners of the greenhouse, which increase fresh air circulation inside. Switch off the fans in the winter to conserve heat.

You should also consider a watering system or piping system. Make sure you properly install the water system and that it works as desired. You must also do frequent maintenance on the pipes to ensure no leaks.

Weed Control

Weeds growing in the greenhouses and other covered structures is one of the most persistent problems that many farmers face. These weeds affect the quality of plants grown, and other types of weeds can act as hosts for pests like whiteflies, snails, mites, and slugs.

Weeds that grow under the benches inside the greenhouse will usually host some pests and fungi; therefore, you need to come up with mechanisms to control the weed growth.

Removing the weed from the greenhouse benches, pots, and even the floor is important in the management of the greenhouse and maintenance of its aesthetic. A ground cloth put under the benches is highly recommended for weed management.

An accumulation of potting media on the ground can appear that will act as the perfect environment for weed growth if you do not collect it. A ground cloth can make it easy to collect the spilled potting media and prevent any germination of weed seeds.

GREENHOUSE

Weeds that have already grown under the benches may force you to have to use herbicide to help manage them. There is a wide variety of herbicides in the market, but the majority of them are for outdoor use, while very few are for indoor use. Don't be tempted to buy the ones labelled for use outdoors, as it may have negative effects to the crops grown inside. In extreme cases, it can affect you plants in the next season. Vapor from some of the traditional herbicides can be trapped inside the structure and will not only affect the crops, but they could also be a health hazard to the people working in the greenhouse.

When applying greenhouse herbicides on the benches, read the instructions carefully. There are two types of herbicides in the greenhouse: **Pre-emergence activity** and **Marengo**. You can apply the herbicide labelled "pre-emergency activity" when the crop is present, and you can water the plant pot even after application. You should not apply BareSpot herbicides on the pot.

You cannot use Marengo herbicide when the plant is present; instead, apply Marengo herbicide before the start of the next growing season. Watering the area with the applied herbicide activates its residual compound, which can damage plants in the area due to volatilization from the herbicide.

Prevention Measures

GREENHOUSE

You should come up with weed management program that allows you to regularly monitor the potting, plant holding, propagation, and the surrounding areas for the presence of weeds.

Before removing the weeds, identify the weed type, its life cycle, and the area where its growing. Always make sure to manually remove weeds from the pots and benches after the plants flower and produce seeds.

The best weed control measure is through weed **sanitation**; that is, keeping away any weed propagules (like seeds, and rhizomes) in the greenhouse structure by using sterile media and cleaning plant materials. You should also control weeds growing outside the greenhouse.

Building concrete floors or having mulched floors will limit weed growth on the floors.

You can manually pull the weeds and prevent them from reaching the seed area in the greenhouse too. Mow the outside to control the weeds outdoors.

Use weed block fabric, which will act as a physical barrier to prevent weed establishment on the floor or under the benches.

You should also use weed-free potting soil. If the container or planting pots spill the potting media, clean them.

In areas where weeds continue to be a problem, you can remove the soil in that area or cover the area with mulch to prevent growth of the weeds.

Weed Management

Managing the weed growing conditions is essential for every greenhouse. A weed-free environment reduces the need for pesticides and increases production of high quality crops. Proper weed control practices help keep pests, insects, and weed diseases at bay.

Weeds compete with your crops for light, water, and nutrients; therefore, you should remove them as soon as possible before they affect your crops' growth. These weeds carry their own viruses too, which can damage or infect your crops.

A weed management program will help you to manage and control the weeds in your greenhouse effectively while helping you come up with control measures.

Sources of Weed Seeds

Weeds come from a variety of sources, some of which include:

- Ventilation fans blowing weed seeds from outside into the greenhouse.

- Contaminated seeds.

- Infected plants transplanted in the greenhouse from an external source.

- Poor plant growing area and storage or using dirty pots and containers.

- Contaminated or uncovered soil from under tables and benches.

- From the irrigation systems and water ponds.

How to Prepare Your Greenhouse for the Winter Season

Winter comes with slow activities after a productive summer. After the spring rush and the summer harvest, the actions you take on your greenhouse will determine how easy your next year's spring period rolls around.

GREENHOUSE

If you want to reduce the amount of work during the next spring frenzy, you have to start preparing your garden for the winter.

To prepare for the winter, there are various things you need to check:

1. Move Out harvested Plants and Tools

Fruits and vegetables that you have already harvested need move out of the greenhouse to create more room for the subsequent season plants.

You should take any pots, containers, seed trays, or any other tools that you are not currently using out for cleaning. Give them a proper scrubbing to remove all the dirt before taking them back to the greenhouse.

Once you have moved out everything out from the greenhouse, clean the structure itself. If you have been planting directly in the greenhouse soil, remove it and replace it with fresh soil and new compost. Doing this helps eliminate any unwanted weed seeds, pests, insects, and diseases established in the soil.

2. Removing Rotten Plants and Weeds

Remove all rotting plants in the greenhouse. Pests and insects feed on the crops during the summer period, and they may lay eggs on the plants or on its leaves; therefore, removing these plants and leaves from the soil will help you get rid of pests.

If the fallen plant leaves are disease-free, you can deposit them in the garden trench and convert them to organic matter.

Remove all established weeds from your structure. You can dig them up and burn them outside. Some invasive weeds remain in the compost matter, so avoid moving the compost from one area of the garden to another.

3. Cleaning the Inside Out

Thorough cleaning of the greenhouse is crucial. If there are still plants in the greenhouse, move them to a warm area and scrub all corners of the structure. You can use hot water and Jeyes fluid disinfectant, which is greenhouse-friendly. Make a plastic dirt-clicking tool to enable you flick dirt from the frames.

You should clean both the inside and outside of the greenhouse, as it not only makes your greenhouse sparkle cleans, but it also allows more light and warmth to enter the greenhouse.

After cleaning, leave the door and windows open to allow fresh air in and so the greenhouse can dry out fast.

4. Moving Tools Inside

Once the inside of the greenhouse is dry, you can return all the greenhouse tools you took out for cleaning (pots, trays, and containers). Then, you can decide what to do with the greenhouse.

You can move frost-sensitive plants inside to give them more warmth during the winter months, especially if you have a heated greenhouse. If you don't have a heated greenhouse, you can provide more warmth to the plants by using bubble wrap.

5. Prepare the Soil for the Spring

Fall is the best time to prepare your soil while you wait for the spring season. You can do this through adding compost, manure, and rock phosphate, among other substances to the soil to boost its nutrients and texture.

You don't have to wait until spring to enrich the soil with the required nutrients. It also helps in improving the drainage system before the busy season.

After preparing the soil and making all the adjustments, you can cover the area with a plastic sheet to prevent heavy winter rains from washing away the soil amendments.

6. Planting Cover Crops

During this period, you can sow cover crops, which helps prevent soil erosion in the area and increase organic matter in the soil bed. Planting cover crops increases nutrients in the soil, so for example, planting legumes or field peas will add to the level of nitrogen in the soil.

7. Trim Perennial Plants

The fall season is the best for pruning perennial plants in the garden. Although this depends on the kind of plant, raspberry plants continue to grow into the winter, whereas you are better off trimming blueberry plants during spring. You can trim herbs like rosemary and thyme during the fall. Blackberries can also benefit from the winter cleaning.

8. Regenerate Compost

After the summer harvest, you can use the compost material from the harvested plant trees and leaves to enrich the garden bed. This increases soil nutrients and can solve soil deficiencies. This practice will make your work easier as you jumpstart to the busy spring period.

Cleaning used compost in the garden makes way for new compost with more active microorganisms and green matter.

9. Adding Mulch to the Soil

Mulching helps prevent water loss by improving soil drainage, preventing soil erosion, and preventing the growth of weeds in your garden. Winter mulching helps regulate soil temperature and retain moisture. As the weather changes, the soil transitions to match the cold weather. The earth freezing can affect the plant roots; therefore, adding mulch to the soil will help regulate the temperature and save the plants' roots from freezing the Earth's surface.

If you have vegetables left in the garden during the fall season, you can add a layer of mulch to the vegetable root soil and prolong the crops' growth.

10. Review the Growing Season

This practice requires you to review the performance of the fruits and vegetables planted during the season. You would evaluate which fruit trees did better based on the produce, and which fruit did well. From this information, you can discern the kinds of fruits and vegetables to grow in your next season.

You will also know which crops to add to the greenhouse to extend your harvest. You can choose to add crops that ripen early or late.

When comparing the performance to choose the next type of vegetables to plant, take notes on what worked for you and what didn't work and check what caused failure or success for each plant.

11. Maintenance of Tools

You may find it difficult to do maintenance on equipment during the busy seasons. During the fall, however, you can clean and remove debris from all your garden equipment. Remove rust with sandpaper, oil them, and sharpen the shovels with a mill file. Oiling the tools helps extend the tools' lifespans.

Chapter Summary

In this chapter, we learned about the different ways to clean the greenhouse and how to maintain the correct temperatures for your fruits and vegetables' success. We went over the various of managing and maintaining a greenhouse.

The chapter highlighted weed management techniques, how weeds can encourage pests and insects, the sources of weeds, how to control weeds established in the greenhouse, along with prevention measures.

From the chapter, you now know various strategies for managing your greenhouse garden during the winter season and how to prepare the garden for the next spring.

In the next chapter, you will learn more about pests and diseases control.

CHAPTER EIGHT

PESTS AND DISEASE CONTROL

One of the major problems many greenhouse farmers face is controlling pests and diseases in their gardens. Pests and diseases can affect plant production, so knowing how to manage these pests and control the spread of diseases can help for a more profitable farm.

Pest Management

Pests are any unwanted organisms in the greenhouse. Pests can affect the normal functioning of plants, and they include weeds, algae, spider mites, insects, and any other organism that can damage plants in the greenhouse.

Many farmers come up with an integrated pest management program to help them solve the problems they have in their farms. Coming up with an integrated disease management system will enable you to identify a wide range of measures you can use to control and prevent all types of diseases.

For any prevention measures to take place, you need to identify the potential infection to the crops. Doing this step will minimize the risk of infection and reduce the spread of the disease to other crops.

Integrated pest management involves coming up with a set of practices to manage and control pests. Controlling pests in the farm will enable you to have healthy and productive crops. Pests and diseases can affect the normal functioning and development of the crop, so controlling these pests and diseases will make the crop more productive.

Conditions Necessary for Disease Occurrence

- Presence of a pathogen.
- Favorable environmental conditions for the pathogen to survive.
- Plant susceptibility to the disease.

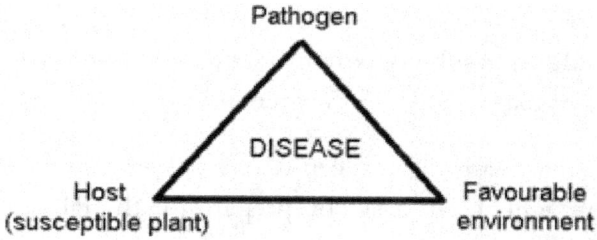

In the disease and pest control triangle, if you can control one or more of these conditions, you are a step closer to controlling the pest (pathogen).

You can control pests in the farm either through the use of pesticides or maintaining good hygiene in the farm. Changing the environmental conditions so they are unfavorable to the pathogen will limit its growth. You can also plant pest resistant crops in the farm.

Maintaining Greenhouse Hygiene

Maintaining the hygiene of the greenhouse is one of the most effective methods you can use to keep pathogens at bay. All the containers, pots, materials, and any other equipment brought inside the greenhouse should be clean.

Installing a foot bath is also essential, especially when dealing with a commercial greenhouse. You should maintain the foot bath and change the disinfectant solution often, as this will minimize the risk of pathogens into the greenhouse.

Alternatively, you can empty the greenhouse and thoroughly clean it as you prepare for the fall season or between crops. Full cleaning of the structure helps remove any pathogens and diseases in the soil compost.

Use Disease-Free Plants

One source of pests is through contaminated seeds. Always buy seeds from trusted sources to avoid bringing pests to your farm through this medium.

When buying seedlings for transplant in your garden, inspect them upon delivery. If you are satisfied and they are disease-free, you can take them inside your greenhouse. Always make sure the storage area is clean and store the seedlings as they await transplant.

If any of the delivered seedlings looks infected, put it in a sealed plastic bag and take it for further testing. Do not plant any infected or potentially infected plants to avoid a spread of pests and diseases to the rest in your greenhouse.

You should also plant pest resistant crops. Most crops are tolerant to downy mildew and powdery mildew diseases.

Control the Growing Environment

Making the conditions unfavorable for the pest to survive in the greenhouse environment is the most effective method of pest control. Controlling the temperature and humidity limits the replication of diseases in the greenhouse.

Monitor the plants regularly to identify any early infection of the plants. This will enable you to take control measures before the pathogens completely damage the plant or spread across the entire greenhouse.

You should throw away pruned material or any other crop residual. Don't leave them to pile in the greenhouse—put all pruned material into disposal bags and throw them out, away from the greenhouse to avoid creating a breeding environment for pathogens. Immediately bury any crop debris from the greenhouse.

Remove weeds growing inside and outside the greenhouse, as weeds can provide a breeding place for pests, insects, and diseases. Removing weeds will help control insects that carry diseases into your plants.

Control Entry to the Greenhouse

You will find most greenhouse pests near doorways, as people can carry these pests and pathogens with them on their clothes and shoes while they walk around. Limit access to the greenhouse, so only a few people can enter.

If there are people visiting your greenhouse, give them disposable overalls to wear and let them pass through the installed foot bath. Avoid inviting visitors coming directly from other farms into your own farm because they may carry a lot of pathogens from their farm and bring them to yours.

Visitors should move from the young and healthy plants in the greenhouse to the older plants. This reduces the risk of spreading pathogens through the greenhouse.

Tips for Pest and Disease Control

1. Determine the Vulnerability of the Plants

Monitor your crops to know when they are vulnerable to pathogens. For example, bacterial diseases affect crops when their leaves sprout out, but they are less likely to affect the plant after the latter's maturity or propagation stage. Crops are also vulnerable to diseases when in the storage room awaiting to be shipped.

2. Determine Which Biocontrol Agents are Suitable for Your Farm

You should know the best biocontrol agent to use for all your gardening operations. Different biocontrol agents affect pests in different ways; therefore, choosing the best biological control will help you control the pests in your garden.

3. Sanitation of the Greenhouse

You should prioritize your greenhouse's sanitation as a defense mechanism against all pests and pathogens. Sanitation involves cleaning the structure to avoid the spread of diseases, removing all plant debris, and weeding the inside and outside of the structure.

4. Choose the Right Insecticide.

There are different types of insecticides used for pest management. Before choosing which type of insecticide to use, determine the common pest problems you face in the greenhouse, when you harvest, and your ultimate plant produce goal. This will help you choose the correct insecticide for your needs.

5. Establish Consistency in Pest Control

Be consistent in pest control measures, as this will lead to a reduced cost for maintaining the greenhouse. It also ensures you can keep an ideal temperature and humidity within the structure.

Integrated Pest Management Techniques

Integrated pest management includes a systematic approach to solving pest issues in the farm. It provides long-term prevention mechanisms and control measures for handling pests and other pathogens in the farm.

These approaches include:

- Monitoring pest infestation.
- Identifying the types of pests in the farm.
- Coming up with control measures.
    - Biological control
    - Chemical control
    - Sanitation

- Mechanical control measures
- Follow up/evaluation.

Monitoring Pest Infestation

This step involves assessing the pest infestation in the farm. It also determines potential pest infestations on your plants. Always do a thorough assessment each day to determine the status of the crops based on its appearance. Keep note of the appearance of the plant and any slight change, and you should also know the signs or symptoms of various potential pests. Daily monitoring of the plants is the key to coming up with early prevention measures.

Identify the Type of Pests Affecting the Crops

When pests infest crops they damage the normal functioning of the crop. Similar to weeds, pests inside the greenhouse compete with the plants for water, light, and nutrients. Different pests affect plants differently; therefore, the plant damage or injury will depend on the type of pest infested in the plant. These pests can include:

1. Insects and Spiders

Insects eat on the plant leaves and other parts of the plant. They also nest on the plants' parts and are often invisible. It's important to know how each pest affects the plant to know which signs to look for in determining the type of pest you are dealing with.

2. Diseases

Some common diseases affecting plants in the greenhouse include: fungi, viruses, and bacteria.

3. Environmental Conditions

Some environmental conditions are favorable to the growth and spread of pathogens within the greenhouse, and different environmental conditions encourage different pest infestations in the greenhouse. Some conditions include:

- Little or too much water.
- Little or too much light.
- Nutrient deficiency in the soil and phytotoxicities.

4. Weeds

The presence of weeds in the greenhouse will cause deficiencies in the crops sown. It competes for nutrients with the crops, limiting the amount of nutrients a plant needs to grow.

Weeds also provide a conducive environment for breeding pests. Always come up with consistent weed control and prevention mechanisms in the greenhouse. Weeds such as prostrate spurge and woodsorrel affect plant produce.

5. Algae

This is a dangerous that affects the people working in the greenhouse; however, it doesn't have any effect on the crops.

6. Snails and Slugs

Snails and slugs affect the younger crops in the greenhouse, and they eat the soft parts of the plants.

7. Nematodes

Nematodes affect the roots of the plant, as they make the roots of the crop swell and knot.

Control Measures

After monitoring the crops and identifying pests affecting them, the next step is to come up with control measures to solve these issues. You can take action that is: biological, chemical, mechanical, or with sanitation processes.

Biocontrol Measures/Biological Controls

Biocontrol measures rely on the use of biological agents to control the growth of pests in the greenhouse. These agents are safer than chemical agents and they include plants, animals, and microbes.

They have some beneficial organisms such as predatory insects and microorganisms, and fungi, and you can use any of these predators to control pests in the greenhouse. Biocontrol has less of an impact on the environment.

Chemical Control Measures

This method uses products with chemicals such as pesticides and insecticides to control pests. There are two types of pesticides: those labelled for general use and those labelled for restricted use.

You can buy the general use pesticide at any garden retail center, and they will be safe to use within your greenhouse. Restricted use pesticides are restricted to use under the supervision of a certified applicator. Its uses are also restricted.

Mechanical Control Measures

Mechanical control processes use hands-on and exclusion methods to control pests; that is, handpicking and destroying the pests in the greenhouse.

Exclusion processes involve closing the doors to ensure pests don't enter inside the greenhouse.

Cultural/Sanitation Processes

Sanitation methods of pest control ensure the environmental conditions are unfavorable for breeding of pests. Having a well-organized, clean, and sanitized environment is an effective way of managing pests. Ensure there is proper temperature control measures, a watering system, and a good fertilization of plants.

Follow-Up/Evaluation

In this step, you take a record of all the methods used in assessing, identifying the pests, and the actions taken. This information is valuable and you can use it to make future decisions in terms of pest management.

Rules for Pesticide Application

When using pesticides, always follow the instructions on the product label. Pesticides are harmful to humans and the environment; therefore, failure to follow those instructions and directions can be hazardous.

You should also warn the workers or people who have access to the greenhouse prior to the application. The warning can be oral or written, and you would use it a protective mechanism for those accessing the greenhouse.

Giving an oral followed by a written warning in highly recommended. You should notify employees about when the pesticide application will take place, instructions not to enter the treated area, and for how many days.

You can put warning signs in areas where everyone can see. If you applied the pesticide in certain sections, there should be a clear description of the treated area or section, and the information for when employees can resume access to those areas.

When applying pesticides, ventilation is crucial. Open the vents while you are spraying the plants, so the fresh air concentration inside is equivalent to the inhalation exposure level as stated on the product label.

Managing Diseases

Managing greenhouse diseases requires proper diagnosis of the diseases and pathogens that have infected your plants, where they came from, and the pathogen biology process. This information will guide you in choosing the right fungicide or pesticide to control the pathogen.

Fungicides manage the spread of diseases in the greenhouse. There are two types: those that act as protectants and those that work as eradicants or are curative.

Protectant fungicides work on the surface of the plant and gets into contact with the pathogen to destroy or control it. Plants require a regular protectant spray application for protection and growth. This type of fungicide can control a wide range of fungal diseases.

On the other hand, plants absorb **eradicant fungicide**. The chemicals control pathogens some distance away from where it landed on the plant. Unlike protectants, you should not apply eradicant as often, as continued use of these pesticides can lead to resistance in the fungal population.

Be careful when spraying pests in the greenhouse because bacteria and some fungi can spread by a moving spray mist, which forms after applying the pesticide. If some pathogens are resistant, then spraying them will only complicate the situation.

Common Sources of Diseases

The common pathogen sources include:

- Infested soil or potting mixture.
- Pathogens from the previously infected crops.
- All-year plants.
- Infected water.
- Pathogen spread through the air.

GREENHOUSE

Infested Soil

Many pathogens and plant diseases in the soil. When you use infested soil in the potting mixture, nutrients in the plants will activate these pathogens; therefore, you should always make sure the potting mix is free from any pathogens before planting your crops. Treat the mixture to kill all the diseases before planting crops on it and ensure you keep all the potting media, benches, shelves, and other tools clean.

Soil from the surface or under benches may also be contaminated, and you should take care to ensure this soil doesn't come into contact with the potting mix.

Debris From Previously Infected Crops

Sometimes, when the conditions are not favorable for survival of pathogens such as extreme temperature or lack of adequate moisture, the pathogens can stay dormant in dead plant leaves, the stem, or on the roots. The dead plant tissues protect the pathogens from the harsh conditions and surface once more when the conditions are favorable.

Some fungi and bacteria can survive for several months in the plant debris. Leaving the infested debris inside the greenhouse may cause the disease to recur.

All-Year Plants

All-year plants in the greenhouse can act as the hosts for pathogens. Viruses and other pathogens depend on living plants to grow and reproduce; therefore, keeping all-year plants in the greenhouse can be a reservoir for these viruses to sprout out from whenever the conditions are favorable for their growth.

Water

Water is the leading cause of pathogens such as pythium. These pathogens make the roots and stem of the plant rot. Water from the lakes, rivers, and ponds may be contaminated with various fungi and bacteria, and once you use them for irrigation, they can bring these pathogens into the greenhouse.

Air

In some cases, pathogens are brought into the greenhouse by air currents from outside plants. Infected plants and weeds near your greenhouse can be the source of pathogens, and it is difficult to prevent floating organisms carried by water. However, you can create an unfavorable environment within the greenhouse to prevent the survival of the disease-causing pathogens.

Make sure to clear the grass and weeds near your greenhouse. Use herbicides outside the greenhouse with caution, as their vapors can be drawn into the greenhouse by fans and air currents and can affect your plants.

Disease Preventive Measures

To control diseases in the greenhouse, you need proper sanitation and a keen eye. Pay a lot of attention to the growth of the crops and note down any slight change. You may have health problems and sudden bacteria growing inside from air infecting the plants. Without preventing measures and preparation, even the tiniest disease can cause huge damage to the crops.

It is not easy to get rid of fungus and bacteria that are affecting your crops quickly, but you can minimize the risk the bacteria will have in your greenhouse.

You can minimize the risk through:

- Proper sanitization of containers, potting media, shelves, stands, and any other tools you use inside the greenhouse.

- Clean the greenhouse surfaces regularly. This can help prevent spore germination in the structure.

- Monitor the temperatures and humidity inside and ensure the greenhouse environment is not prone to disease.

- Ensure there is proper ventilation by increasing the supply of fresh air circulation inside.

- Make sure there is enough space between the plants to increase air circulation around them.

- Avoid water splashing on your plants; only water them at the base or on their crowns.

- Monitor new seedlings to ensure they are disease-free.

- Check the crops daily for any signs of disease, discolorations, or any other symptoms.

Common Greenhouse Diseases

There are various common diseases you may come across while tending to your garden. Some of the sources include infected plants from outside, carried in by insects or floating in the air. The following sections will outline some of these diseases in more detail.

Fungus

Wet conditions or overwatering can cause fungus diseases like phytophthora, powdery mildew, root rot, and botrytis. You should monitor the moisture and humidity level in the greenhouse to avoid conditions that favor breeding of fungus.

Ensure there is proper drainage of containers and other potting media and do not leave plants soaked in water for a long time.

When fungi infect plants, the plants start to wilt and discolor. Sometimes, they may have fuzzy growth on their stem and leaves, which may later turn yellow in color. If the infections affect only the surface of the plant, you can apply neem oil and increase air circulation in the area. If the fungi affect the plant tissue, you should remove the plants from your garden and discard them far away. It is difficult to treat tissue-affected plants.

Bacterial Diseases

Some bacterial diseases that affect plants include Erwinia and bacterial blight. It is not easy to cure these diseases, and if they infect your plants, you will have to get them out of the garden and destroy them immediately.

The infected plants will have water-soaked spots while its tissue melts into a sticky mess. If you notice any of these signs, remove them right away.

Bacterial diseases can spread to other plants through dirty tools, potting medium, and containers. Proper sanitation and increased air circulation are important factors in preventing the spread of bacterial diseases.

Viruses

Viruses occur in various forms and sizes and are brought inside the greenhouse by insects (thrips and aphids), which are classified as plant-feeding insects. Plants infected by a virus have a yellow color or mosaic patterns on their leaves. If you notice any signs of a virus infection on your plants, you should take them out and destroy them immediately.

Always monitor your greenhouse for insects and treat your plants when they appear as soon as possible.

For any pest and disease control mechanisms to succeed, you must:

- Understand the various components of greenhouse diseases.

- Understand the different sources of the diseases you're facing; that is, are they caused by organisms or influenced by the conditions in the greenhouse?

- Understand the different symptoms of all the pathogens. Know signs of root rot, symptoms of bacteria and virus affected plants and those of mildews, as knowing them will help you decide which pesticide or control mechanism to apply.

- Know the resistance mechanisms of the pests and fungi.

To control root rots in the greenhouse, you need to:

- Remove the infected crops.

- Sterilize the potting media.

- Wash your hands with soap to avoid spreading pathogens to other areas.

- Control the irrigation system to have a moderate soil moisture. The potting medium used should have adequate drainage to avoid waterlogged crops, and you should also make sure you are not overwatering the crops.

- Use the right fungicides to prevent seedling infections.

You would control powdery mildew pests by:

- Reducing the greenhouse's humidity.
- Removing dead plant debris or material.
- Using fungicides to prevent the spread of infections.

If the irrigation water is the one causing pathogens, you should decontaminate the water through chemical treatment, filtration, or an irradiation method.

Chapter Summary

Controlling pests and insects affecting your crops in the greenhouse increases the productivity of the crops. Farmers use integrated pest management techniques to identify the types of pests affecting the farms and come up with the appropriate methods to control and prevent those pests.

You can solve most pathogen problems by maintaining good greenhouse hygiene, using disease-free plants, controlling the growing environment, and controlling entry to the greenhouse.

Other control methods you can implement include using biocontrol and chemical control and sanitizing the greenhouse environment. Successful control of pests and diseases requires you not only to discern the pest or disease affecting the plants, but also know the symptoms for each disease.

Diseases in the greenhouse are attributed to various sources of living organisms. Although there are other sources, these are the most common when figuring out the cause of pathogens and diseases in the greenhouse. Every greenhouse farmer should know the various sources and use that knowledge to come up with measures on how to prevent these pathogens.

In the next chapter, you will learn about various mistakes to avoid.

CHAPTER NINE

MISTAKES TO AVOID

The success of the farm produce is the dream of every farmer. However, there are many mistakes most beginners make when cultivating fruits and vegetables in their garden.

Learning about the mistakes that others made will help you not commit the same when you're in the initial stages of your gardening activities. Learning ahead contributes positively to the success of your farm and enables you to harvest healthier and tastier plants.

Site Selection

You cannot set a greenhouse in just any random place—you need to identify a good spot with a good drainage system. An area with a good slope is ideal for draining water in the greenhouse, and the greenhouse floor should be porous to allow water to drain properly. Floors made of gravel will do well in draining water.

A poor drainage system will result in waterlogged areas, which will be a breeding place for pests and other diseases that can affect your plants.

Setting Up the Greenhouse Away from Excess Shade

You must build your greenhouse in an area that receives less shade from tall trees and other buildings around. Excess shade will limit lighting, which is essential for plant growth in the greenhouse. Tree branches may also fall on the greenhouse and cause serious damage.

Plants also need protection from extreme heat during the summer months; therefore, installing a greenhouse that has shading material to shade the plants from the hot sun is a much better idea than placing a greenhouse otherwise.

Choosing the Right Plant to Grow in the Garden

You need to choose the right plant to grow in the greenhouse; for example, growing fruits together with vegetables may affect them. Fruit plants' height cause shade, which can affect the growth of other vegetables or crops grown in the same greenhouse. You must make sure you grow your fruits and other tall plant trees separately from other plants and vegetables.

Note that not all plants do well in a greenhouse, and some plants will need an open field to maximize their yield.

Humidity Inside the Greenhouse

High levels of humidity will encourage growth of mold spores and other diseases, which will affect your plants. You need to know the humidity needs of your plants and control the humidity level in the greenhouse to favor your plants' growth. Plants that need the same humidity levels should be growth on the same section.

Place Growing Bags and Pots in a Garden Stand

Putting growing bags, pots, and other basic greenhouse tools on the floor can encourage the growth of pests beneath the pots and growing bags. Garden stands allow you to arrange your pots on a double or triple step stand, thus creating more space in your greenhouse. Using stands can help you maintain good hygiene within the greenhouse.

You should always adhere to proper hygiene in the greenhouse to discourage weeds and pest infections from growing and becoming issues.

Excess Watering

Avoid overwatering plants in the greenhouse, as the humidity inside is controlled and there will be less water evaporation from the greenhouse soil. The excess water on the plants will encourage fungal infections and other diseases in the greenhouse.

Follow proper watering schedules and create a set watering schedule for yourself, in which you water at the same time every day.

Poor Pollination or No Pollinators Inside the Greenhouse

You have to plant floral plants near your greenhouse to attract pollinators to the surrounding area and eventually to your garden. Pollinators are attracted to the color yellow, so planting plants like marigold will attract them.

In some cases, there may be few to no insect pollinators in the greenhouse, thus affecting the pollination process. In this situation, hand pollination is essential for pollinating vegetable plants.

Failure to Expose the Garden Soil to Direct Sunlight

You need to expose the soil and the potting mixture to direct sunlight; otherwise, it will attract pests and maggots into the greenhouse. Exposing the soil inside to direct sunlight will kill most of these pests and fungal diseases. Don't make the mistake of leaving your soil out of the sun, especially if you are in an urban area. Make sure there is direct sunlight to kill the pests in the soil.

Pest Management

Most farmers don't pay close attention to their vegetables and plants and they fail to notice the slight changes in their plant until the pest has already damaged some plants and spread to other parts. Daily monitoring is essential to identify and pest infestation at its initial stages. This will make it easier to identify any infection and take appropriate measures before it spreads to other plants.

Crop Rotation

Another mistake many farmers make is planting the same crop in the same place for several seasons. Crop rotation is essential for success of any farm production. After harvesting a single crop, plant a different crop in that location, as this will help retain the soil's fertility and nutrients, resulting in healthy plants.

Heating

Don't buy the regular home heater for your greenhouse, as home heaters are not designed for moist environments. Buy rated heaters specifically designed for greenhouse and use them to regulate the winter temperatures. You should also use a rated power cord and an outdoor surge protector.

Fertilizers

Before applying any fertilizer to your plants, study the feeding patterns of the plants and its requirements. Each plant has different requirements beyond the general all-purpose fertilizer. Vegetables need fertilizer specifically formulated for use in the greenhouse. For example, tomatoes require a specific amount of fertilizer that is made for them, and how you would apply that fertilizer will depend on the instructions on the product label. Your studies will guide you in applying the right fertilizer and the right amount of fertilizer.

If you have several plants in your garden, group them based on their needs (water, shade, and fertilizer). You should also note down the feeding requirements of the plants and mark them. You may learn of some plants that require a lot of shade, but their fertilizer requirement is different from the others in the same group. Studying your plants' requirements early, even before the growing season, will result into a successful garden and healthy plants.

Determine the fertilizer pH level. Tomatoes grown in a container require a pH level that ranges from 5.6 to 5.8 for maximum yield. A high or low pH level will affect the nutrient value in the crops and will also limit the plants from achieving their maximum yield potential.

Rely on a Problem Resolution Center

If you face challenges in your garden, you should ask for help from a professional educator. Taking pictures of the infected crops will help in the documentation of the problem and makes it easy for the educator to give advice if they can't make it personally to your garden.

Commercial greenhouses require you to hire an agronomist to come and investigate your farm on a monthly basis. Always seek for help or assistance if you notice something with your plants.

Chapter Summary

If you're growing your own fruits, vegetables, and herbs to share with your family, there is more to cultivating these crops in a greenhouse. Knowing all the greenhouse mistakes to avoid is a great way to begin you gardening journey.

Continuous learning and improvement of your gardening activities will result to gardening success and eventually a healthy harvest.

FINAL WORDS

Greenhouse structures are essential to extend the growing period. Whether building a greenhouse to plant crops for personal use or commercial use, there are a lot of benefits you can get. Before building a greenhouse, there are various factors you have to consider like site planning and the types of plants to have in the greenhouse.

Depending on your location, you have to choose the right place to install the greenhouse. The site you select should have a good drainage system and be away from excess shade. After site planning, you need to choose the type of greenhouse to install. There are various designs with different styles and sizes, so choose a greenhouse type based on your plants' needs, budget, and the location. Set up a good layout for the greenhouse for how you want to arrange the sections.

Once you install your greenhouse, the next step is to add all the necessary equipment required for its operation. When dealing with different plants, you will notice each plant requires different climate conditions such as heating, temperature, and lighting. If you're planning to have all-year-round crops and extend the growing season, having an enclosed structure will be ideal. Greenhouses allow the farmer to control climatic conditions and humidity to make the environment suitable for cultivating vegetables, herbs, and fruits at any time.

To control climatic conditions in the structure, you need to invest in lighting system equipment, ventilation equipment, temperature control, and heating equipment. You also need to have the basic equipment for operating the greenhouse, which includes pots, containers, and trays for planting seeds. You need to place these pots on shelves or in the greenhouse benches to create more space for other plants.

Remember to water the pots and seedling trays well for the seeds to germinate. A good water management system is essential in your structure, and you can decide to use drip irrigation or an automatic watering system. Whichever system you choose, you have to ensure there is a good drainage system to avoid having a waterlogged condition. Poor drainage may harbor pests and diseases in the greenhouse, and to an extreme extent, result in rotting of the plant roots.

Once you have placed all the equipment, tools, and accessories, you can go ahead and start cultivating your plants. You need to get seed-starting mixture to plant the seeds. Avoid using the normal potting soil, which may be infested with pests and other pathogens.

Soil preparation is essential when deciding on what plants to plant, and vegetables and fruits will do well in different types of soil; therefore, you need to determine which type of soil is suitable for planting each.

Soil preparation involves determining the type of soil and its consistency, how to improve the soil drainage, determining soil nutrients and pH level, balancing the pH level, and adding more nutrients to the soil through fertilization. Based on this information, you can figure out which soil is suitable for your plants. The water requirements for your vegetables or herbs depends on the type of soil in your garden. Water your plants with care and avoid overwatering or underwatering them.

Once the seeds germinate, you may decide to transplant the seedlings to a bigger container or put them to their final growing place. As the plants grow, you can add mulch to boost the plant nutrients and prevent weeds from growing. Monitor the plants growth on a daily basis to identify any change on the plant leaves. Watching the plants daily will in noting the plants' progress and identifying any pests or diseases that may infect the crops. The information you gather can help you know when to remove infected crops before they spread the disease.

Pollination is essential for the production of the plants. Most greenhouses lack pollinators, so hand pollination will be important for your plants to produce fruits. Alternatively, you can plant crops that attract bee pollinators around your greenhouse and open the windows to allow them to enter inside to pollinate your plants. Insect-pollinated plants produce more fruit compared to self-pollinated plants, and different vegetables, fruits, and herbs rely on different methods of pollination to produce fruits.

For all the plants to give you the maximum yield, you must have proper management of the greenhouse. Different plants do well in different seasons, so always know which type of vegetable of fruit you can grow in summer or during the busy spring season. Knowing when and what to plant during each season will play a huge part in your greenhouse's success. You also need to know how you can prepare your greenhouse for the winter season.

Proper maintenance of the greenhouse involves maintaining good greenhouse hygiene, weed control, and pest and disease management. You need to identify the various pests that can affect your greenhouse, their symptoms in the infected plants, and what causes them. It's only after determining the pest's sources and signs when you can come up with preventive and control procedures.

You should evaluate and document the control procedures you take for future decision-making. Regular monitoring of the crops, fertilization, and watering will result to healthy and productive plants.

You also need to remember the various mistakes others have made before you and that you may face while growing your plants. Learning ahead will enable you to avoid some of these mistakes, and continuous learning and improvement of your gardening activities will result to gardening success, and eventually, a healthy harvest.

www.ingramcontent.com/pod-product-compliance
Lightning Source LLC
Chambersburg PA
CBHW070423010526
44118CB00014B/1885